FOOTBALL FABLES

FOOTBALL FABLES

Iain Macintosh

First published 2008
A & C Black Publishers Ltd
38 Soho Square
London W1D 3HB
www.acblack.com

© 2008 Iain Macintosh

ISBN 978-0-7136-8954-9

A CIP catalogue record for this book is available from the British Library.

Photo of Barry Fry courtesy of PA Archive/PA Photos
Photos of David Icke, Ron Atkinson, Carlton Palmer, Alan Kennedy
courtesy of EMPICS Sport/PA Photos
Photos of Ron Harris, Stan Bowles, Frank McAvennie courtesy of PA Photos
Photos of Espen Baardsen, Bryan Robson, Ramon Vega
courtesy of Getty Images
Photos of Peter Shilton, Nigel Spackman, Nottingham Forest
courtesy of Bob Thomas/Getty Images

A&C Black uses paper produced with elemental chlorine-free pulp,
harvested from managed sustainable forests.

Typeset in Galliard by seagulls.net
Printed and bound by Caligraving Ltd, Thetford, Norfolk

CONTENTS

Acknowledgements

Thanks go firstly to my wonderful girlfriend Rachael Grady who not only convinced me to actually have a crack at doing this, but who also coped with my moods, tantrums, rants and panics when things didn't go according to plan. If it's any consolation, I love you more than you realise.

Likewise, my parents Chris and Heather Macintosh, along with my sister Isla, had to put up with countless phone calls when it all went titsy. Their constant unwavering faith in me is also thoroughly undeserved, but more appreciated than they could possibly imagine.

Thanks to everyone at Icons.com who gave a highly strung bin bag salesman a chance to write again. Enormous amounts of respect to Tom Rollett, James Freedman, Adrian Clarke, Laura Greene and, in particular, to David Holland who came to my rescue with important phone numbers on more than one occasion.

Tony Pearson convinced me that I could do this with the sage advice that, "of course you're going to be able to do it. You'll do it because you can't *not* do it. You're not going to go back to selling bin bags, are you? No, of course you're not. So don't worry. You'll do it."

Toby Fuhrman, Tom Warren, Matt Walker, Matt Gallagher, Dan Bourke, Dave Adams, Shaun Nickless, Jim Findlay and Penny Rance (who mentioned me in her book's acknowledgements, the excellent *Virgin Films – Martial Arts* in case you're interested) were all of great assistance, not just for test-reading but also for advice and, you know, friendship.

Thanks to my publisher, Charlotte Atyeo, and her predecessor Rob Foss, for showing faith in a project that, at first glance, had no discernible commercial benefits. It could not have been completed without Charlotte's wise advice, calm guidance and understated threats of physical violence.

Thanks to Judy Tither for making a number of world-class saves during the proof-reading.

Thanks to Emma Sorensen for the invaluable help putting the synopsis together.

Amelia Durham of Champions PLC was a great assistance in arranging the interview with Peter Shilton.

Tony Clarke came riding to my rescue as well by arranging the interview with Alan Kennedy and if you need ex-footballers for after-dinner speaking, you should really have a look at www.soccerspeakers.com.

Thanks also to everyone at www.shrimperzone.com, TBTV, Sky Sports News and the makers of Football Manager 2007 for being worthy enough distractions to put this project in serious jeopardy on more than one occasion.

But, finally, huge, huge thanks must obviously go to Barry, Espen, Ron, Peter, David, Nigel, Big Ron, Bryan, Ramon, Carlton, Stan, Frank, Alan, Tony and Viv for giving up their time to be interviewed.

INTRODUCTION

Before I do anything else, might I first thank you for taking this book down from the shelf? The chances are that you found it tucked up in the middle of the sports section flanked on one side by a heavily blinged 23-year-old midfielder's autobiography and on the other by an unauthorised look at a 21-year-old who has scored fewer goals for England than Mick Channon. Maybe Channon himself was there as well, but I doubt it somehow.

The market is crammed with glossy, sanitised chronicles that have been so closely monitored by a football agent that you can still smell the aftershave in the binding. It always seems strange when people in their twenties release autobiographies. I thought you were supposed to write your memoirs as you toddled up the garden path towards death's door. Certainly the best I've ever read were the books by the late Brian Clough and the slightly later Sir Stanley Matthews. If I want to read a life story, I would generally go to someone who has lived their life and who might be in a position to bestow snippets of wisdom. If I want to learn how to play tinny, repetitive R&B from a cheap mobile phone, that's when I'll go to a 21-year-old. Besides, what can a current player really say about anyone anyway? Would you write a book hammering your boss or the boss of a rival company if you'd only made two payments to your pension fund? Of course not, you'd be bland and inoffensive just in case anyone else wanted to hire you in the future.

The trouble is that even men at the end of a long and glittering career can write memoirs that are brain-meltingly boring. What I've tried to do here is to avoid both pitfalls and create an anthology of football stories. An antidote to the anodyne. Instead of just one retired footballer telling you about everything he's ever done, I've gone to speak to 15 of them and asked them to simply tell me one story. I hope that a combination of tales, from a selection of characters across a spread of eras, will be more interesting than someone telling you what kind of Ferrari he bought with his signing-on fee. The fact that you've plucked this book from the mêlée indicates that you might feel the same way.

I've attempted to choose as eclectic a mix of interviewees as I could, covering both club and international football from 1970 onwards. I'm afraid this book does not contain shiny, polished recollections of flash-in-the-pan twenty-somethings. It does not contain anything from anyone who has ever invited Atomic Kitten to their 18th birthday party and there are no mentions of Baby Bentleys anywhere. This book contains stories from proper footballers who have achieved great things, both on and off the pitch. Like the traditional fables of old, some of the details in the stories may be sketchily recalled or may have evolved over time through telling and retelling. This book is not an encyclopaedia. This book is all about the stories.

Welcome to Football Fables.

1 ⚽ BARRY FRY
Southend's Great Escape (1993)

Barry Fry arrived for our lunch in Peterborough and strode through the half-empty restaurant to meet me. A dozen heads instantly craned round in interest, for Fry is not a stealthy man. Taller than I first expected and well built, his gravelly laugh echoed around the room and, I'm delighted to report, continued to attract attention throughout the afternoon, particularly when it followed a string of inventive swearwords.

A cult hero for many football fans, Fry is everything you would expect him to be, but slightly louder. There is no off switch, no respite and no hope of a quiet lunch for any of our fellow diners. Unlike some interviewees, he doesn't require any warming up at all. From the first question to the last, he rattles off a string of anecdotes, some of them far too libellous to be included here and all of them crammed with enough expletives to wear out my asterisk button.

Fry has become so synonymous with the dug-out in the last 20 years that many people are surprised to hear that he was a very promising footballer. Unfortunately, he never fulfilled his potential. Plucked from his native Bedford by Sir Matt Busby at a young age, he arrived at Manchester United with high hopes. Despite appearances for the England Schoolboy side, he failed to make the grade at Old Trafford and was released. His career never really got going and he retired at 28.

He blamed himself for this failure, acknowledging that he had been distracted by other interests in spite of Busby's warnings to moderate his behaviour. As a manager, however, he left a far greater mark. From convincing George Best to turn out for non-league Dunstable, to guiding tiny Barnet into the football league, he was a difficult man to ignore. Not only was he successful on a shoestring but his patented goal celebration of haring down the touchline like a firework in a flat cap was a big hit with the press.

Unfortunately, his chairman at Barnet, the notorious ticket tout Stan Flashman, was not always willing to let Fry have his own way. The two men clashed repeatedly, notably on one occasion when the chairman threatened to have his manager buried underneath the M25. Fry once told me that he'd been sacked 38 times by Flashman. Indeed, in Ian Ridley's book *A Season in the Cold*, he is quoted as saying, "He's sacked me at least 20 times and he's meant it. But I've just got up the next morning, gone to the ground and got on with my work, and he's phoned up two or three days later as if nothing has happened. There is going to be a time when he sacks me and really means it."

In the spring of 1993, after 14 years with the club, the uncertainty finally took its toll and Barry Fry ran out of patience with his boss.

I was finished at Barnet as soon as Stan Flashman put lawyers in charge of the club. Now, you have to remember at this stage that the club was so deep in the shit that I'd had to lend them £164,000 of my own money just so it could survive and neither me nor the players had been paid for months. Anyway, I had a meeting with this lawyer. He's come in and said he was taking over the running of the club. Obviously with me being one of the biggest creditors, I said, "Where does this leave me?"

He said, "Well, you're just another creditor."

That didn't make me feel too valued. I told him that I'd just been approached by Vic Jobson, the chairman at Southend, regarding the vacant manager's job and I didn't know whether to take it or not.

He said immediately, "How much will they pay us for your services?"

I says, "Well, as I'm owed £164,000 from this football club, I don't think they'll pay fuck all."

But that was it. It made my mind up. He wasn't bothered about whether I wanted to go or not or anything like that. He was just bothered about how much the club in question wanted to pay for me. After that meeting I rang Vic Jobson, went down to Roots Hall and he offered me the job. Believe it or not, I was appointed as the new Southend Manager on April Fool's Day.

At the time they was bottom of the league with nine games to go. Obviously the transfer deadline had been and gone. Nine games left and I think we was seven points adrift. Vic actually said we was down and I said he was a defeatist and that we'd definitely stay up. He thought I was mad. So mad, he offered me a bonus if we survived! Ha, ha, ha! So that worked out well!

The next day the team was travelling up to Sunderland for a league game. I live in Bedford so my wife drove me to the round-about where the coach would come past and pick me up. I'll never forget getting on that coach. Danny Greaves, my only member of staff and a massive unsung hero throughout that run-in, introduced me to everyone.

You know, "Barry, this is Brett Angell. Barry, this is Stan Collymore," and all that. You know what? Not one of 'em looked me in the eye. They all shook my hand, but they was all staring at the floor. The mood was one of total depression and misery.

So we got to the hotel in Sunderland and I called the lads together. "Right," I said. "We're having a meal together at 7pm, so come down then. You can go back to your rooms afterwards, get yourself suited and booted and then, about 10.30pm, I want you to come down, head off to the nearest nightclub and go chill out. If any of you come back to this hotel before 2am, I'll fine you two weeks' wages."

They looked at me like I was from a different planet!

Anyway, the lads have their food and go upstairs and Vic walks in with a few of the directors.

Vic says, "I'm very impressed, Barry. The lads have gone. Usually they're just hanging around in the corner playing cards."

"Nah," I says, "I've sent them up to their rooms."

So, he's introducing me to a few of the directors and we're sitting around having a chat at about 10.30 and suddenly his face just drops and he starts gaping at something behind me. I turn around and there's all the players trooping out the front door.

"What's going on?" says Vic.

"Oh, that? Yeah, I told the players to go for a walk."

"A walk," says Jobson. "How professional! We've never had that here before. A walk? At 10.30pm! How marvellous. Where are they going?"

I said, "They're going to a nightclub round the corner, Vic. I've told them if they come home early I'll fine them," and I get up and go over to the lads. "No alcohol, lads," I remind them. "Just go out, chill out and relax."

When I came back, Vic and the directors are all up at the bar. Vic walks over to me with a look on his face.

"You alright, Mr Chairman?"

"No, I'm not alright," he says. "Do you know we've got a game tomorrow?"

"Of course I do," I said. "We're playing fucking Sunderland, otherwise we wouldn't be here!"

He says, "You've just sent all of our players to a nightclub! I've never heard of anything so stupid in all my life!"

I says, "Hold on, Vic. What do you normally do on a Friday night when you stay over?"

He says, "Well, we have a meal, then the team play cards and go to bed at 11pm."

"Well, let's be fair, Vic," I said, "it ain't done you much good here, has it? We're bottom of the fucking league!"

I said, "I've come up on the team coach and they're all miserable. They're all demoralised. I've got to get 'em to relax and chill out. I'm sorry, Vic, but this is my way."

He just turned around and walked away. I went up to my room that night wondering if this was going to be the shortest fucking managerial reign of all time.

Fortunately, the next day, we was absolutely fucking brilliant! We won 4–2 at Roker Park and we was sensational. After the game Terry Butcher, the Sunderland manager, comes over and says, "How did you get them to play like that, you're bottom of the league!"

I told him I didn't have a fucking clue! All I'd done was to tell the players before the game that everyone already thought they were relegated, that they had nothing to lose and that they should just go out and enjoy the game. "Even the chairman thinks you're down," I told them, "but I don't."

Four two! Unbelievable! Of course, the players tried to take the piss with me after that. Every away game it was all, "Are we going out to a nightclub, gaffer?"

I never let it happen again though!

On the following Wednesday we had West Ham and they was top

of the league at the time. It's at Roots Hall, full house and the atmosphere is unbelievable. Having come from Barnet, I had no idea about the rivalry between the two clubs. The reception I got from the fans at the beginning of the game was amazing. You'd have thought I was some kind of God from the noise they made when I took my hat off and waved at them. I tell you what, from start to finish, they got behind the lads; it was like a Cup Final that night. To be fair, West Ham absolutely battered us, but we defended well. Then Stan Collymore got it on the outside right, beat three people with his strength and his pace, whipped in a cross and Brett Angell flew in to stab it home. We won 1–0!

All of a sudden from being down and relegated on Thursday night, we've won two and we've got a chance. From Friday night at the hotel in Sunderland when I was 'Shitbag of the Year' to Vic Jobson, suddenly I was a football genius! Really, I was just bloody lucky! Nothing to do with tactics, just about putting a smile on the lads' faces. Trying to get them to believe in themselves.

I suppose in a way it helped that I couldn't buy any new players. Not that we really needed them. I mean, we had some quality players there: Keith Jones, Andy Ansah, Chris Powell, all good footballers. God knows what they were doing at the bottom of the league in the first place. If you've got Brett Angell and Stan Collymore in your frontline, you've always got a chance.

Of course, Stan was playing with a smile on his face back then. I knew all about him when I arrived, I'd try to sign him when I was at Barnet and he was at Stafford Rangers. I'd spoken to him on that first night in Sunderland, because there was a lot of talk of him heading off to Nottingham Forest before the transfer deadline. Nothing had happened in the end and I asked him how he was, whether he was disappointed or not. He was honest to me and he said he was.

I said, "Well listen, Stan. If you do well for me in the remaining nine games, I'll sort it out for you to go wherever you like in the summer. I just want you to concentrate on the football," I said. "I don't want you sulking, I want you to go out and express yourself, enjoy yourself. I'm a man of my word, I'll let you go wherever you want in the summer."

He was brilliant for Southend United. He wasn't just a great goal-scorer; he used to be fantastic on the flanks as well, running into space, crossing it for other people to score. He was a proper football man as well. He thinks very deeply about the game and he used to go watch a lot of matches in his spare time, which isn't usual for a player. When I was manager at Birmingham and he was playing at Aston Villa I used to go and check out opponents and I'd often see him in the stands. The only time I had to give him a bollocking was at Cambridge, the one game we lost in that run-in.

I said to Stan, "You're playing well, you've impressed me. I had a word with Alex Ferguson and I've told him you're the real deal. He's sent a scout down to watch you today, so be sure to impress him." Course, what happens that afternoon? We was fucking hopeless. We got beat 3–1, and it should have been fucking 10–1. Stan's fucking useless and I've slated him at half-time.

I've said, "Stan! I've just told Fergie how good you are! He's sent a fucking scout and the fucker's gone home after 20 minutes because you're fucking rubbish!"

To be fair to Collymore, he held his hand up and took it, but I tell you something about him. His sister was dying of cancer back home in Cannock and when I found out I'd told Stan to have every Monday off so he could get back and see her. After that bollocking though, he was back in training with the rest of the lads. He was annoyed with himself about his performance. I knew then that he'd play at the highest level, because it hurt him so much to play so bad.

Whenever journalists ring me up about Stan, they ask me for a story.

I always say, "When he was at Southend he used to visit local schools and give anti-drugs speeches to the kids."

They'd say, "Nah, not that one."

I'd say, "Alright, when he was at Southend he used to spend his spare time visiting kids in hospitals."

But they don't want those stories, do they? I can only speak as I find, but when Stan Collymore was at Southend United he was fucking brilliant.

So there we are on May 8, going into the final match and we've won six, drawn one and lost that one against Cambridge. We need a win to stay up and who do we face? My old mate David Pleat at Luton Town and he's in exactly the same position!

Me and Pleaty used to play together for England Schoolboys. In fact, one game, he's taken a corner and I've headed it in to score at Wembley in front of 93,000 people. He was always my mate after that!

I remember being nervous before the game and that's not like me. Normally I'm cocky and confident. I think my team's better than the opposition and no matter how many goals they score, I'll fucking score more.

Before the game I sat the players down and spoke to them. "You lads have been marvellous," I said. "You picked yourselves up from an impossible position, you were certs for relegation and you've got yourself here, where you can win and stay up. It's all in your hands now. You've come so far, for fuck's sake, don't let yourselves down now."

I don't remember a thing about the match. It was one of the horrible nervy ones where you kick every ball. The record books say that we scored twice in the first half, but then conceded just before the break, but it's all a blur to me. What I do know is that we eventually held on throughout the second half and when the final whistle went, oh, the relief!

What an occasion! The fans came on to the pitch and it was chaos. Stan got lifted up on people's shoulders, but not before they'd stripped him of everything but his pants! There was just all these players running about in just their little Y-fronts!

Vic Jobson cried at the end of the game. He actually cried. "I never would have believed it," he said. Then he offered me a job for life.

That summer I kept my word and sold Stan to Nottingham Forest. We got £2.25 million plus enough add-ons to make the transfer eventually worth over £4 million. I bought in new players, including Ricky Otto who was an absolute bargain at £100,000. What a player he was. But it wasn't to last.

It all come to a head in December when we was flying high in the league. I was watching Nottingham Forest play Birmingham and I was surprised to find that Vic had come along as well. That's not normal, for a chairman to come and scout future opponents, so I'm a bit concerned.

He's sat next to me in the first half and, after the break, he comes back from the Director's Box and says, "I've just been speaking to Karren Brady [MD of Birmingham] and David Sullivan [co-owner of the club]. They've asked permission to speak to you."

I said, "Really? What did you say?"

He's said, "I've told them they can't!"

I said, "Fair enough."

But I'm uncomfortable for the whole game. "Why's Vic even here?" I thought. "What's going on?"

The next day David Sullivan's run a piece in his own paper [*The Sport*] saying that he wanted Barry Fry and he was going to get him in a room and not let him out until he became Birmingham manager.

So the next game, I'm being interviewed on the telly and Vic's standing behind me. The interviewer's said, "What's the situation with Birmingham City?"

I said, "Well, I've spoken to Vic and I've said, I'd like to speak to them."

And Vic's jumped in on the interview and started with this garbage about not wanting me to go and only allowing Birmingham to speak to me if they give him an undertaking that they won't talk to me about taking the manager's job.

I've gone, "You bleedin' what?" I mean, what *were* they allowed to talk to me about? The weather?

I'm already paranoid anyway, I've got to be honest, because I've been hearing whispers for some time that Vic wants me out and wants Peter Taylor in and I'm thinking, "This fucking geezer's wanting to get rid of me!"

So, I've gone to Birmingham, I've talked to Karren Brady and it's a very ambitious club. Bottom of the league, the stadium's a khazi, but I'm thinking, "It's a sleeping giant and I want to wake it up."

But then I thought, I'll go back to Southend. We're third in the league. Third in the league at Christmas! Let's see what they say and then go from there.

So, I've drove back from Birmingham to Southend that night and there's a board meeting and I told them what I'd been offered.

John Adams, on the board, he says, "Right, what do you want here?"

"Well," I says, "I want a more secure contract than what I've got."

Vic says, "You've got a job for life, I told you that."

I said, "Vic, you've told me I've got a job for life, but the actual reading of the contract says that at any time you can give me six months' money and terminate it. I'm on £55,000 a year, so that's £27,500 and I'm out. That don't sound like a contract for life to me. In reality, Vic, this contract ain't worth the paper it's writ on."

So Vic says, "If you're after more money, you're not getting a fucking penny more."

So, to be fair to John Adams, he says, "Hold on, hold on, hold on. Barry, what do you want?"

I said, "I've told you. I want stability. I've got a flat on the seafront, I've showed my commitment to you, where's your commitment to me? All I've got to do is hit a bad patch and you can say, 'Alright Baz, here's your money, now fuck off'. That ain't a job for life."

He's got up, has Vic, at the other end of the table and he's said, "Barry. I will not give you another fucking penny." And he's walked out!

One director's offered me £30,000 out of his own pocket to stay, asking me to take it and not tell Vic. I said to him, "No disrespect, but that ain't the way to run a football club. I get the feeling that the chairman don't want me to stay, and if that's the case there's a club down the road that want me. And I'm going."

Vic offered no resistance to me leaving whatsoever. The worst thing was that the fans went absolutely bananas. They said I was a Judas, they sent me death threats and I thought, "Do they really know what's happened?"

They're like, "You fucking fat greedy bastard," but it weren't like that at all. Mums and Dads would come over to me with their kids and say, "I used to like you, but I fucking hate you now, you greedy shit."

Well, let me tell you this. When I was at Southend I was on the same transfer revenue deal as all the other managers Vic had hired. Vic was very good, he said, "We're a small club and we've got to sell to survive. I'm going to ask you to sell your best players and if you do that, you stand more of a chance of being sacked. It's only fair that you get a 10 per cent cut when you have to sell them."

Now, on that Collymore deal, remember, we made £4 million, so I've got £400,000 coming to me.

Except I ain't. Because the whole Collymore deal was spread over a long period of time and paid in instalments and as soon as I leave the club, I don't get nothing.

So there's everyone thinking I'm leaving Southend because I'm a fucking, fat, greedy bastard when I could have just sat there and waited for £400,000 to land in my bank account! Greedy bastard? I lost a fucking fortune. Ain't it ironic?

I don't regret nothing though, I loved it at Southend. Nine months of absolute heaven and just that final 24 hours of sadness. But I'll never, as long as I live, understand why Vic made no attempt to keep me there.

Barry Fry left Southend United for St Andrews in the winter of 1993. Birmingham were marooned at the bottom of the table and he immediately set about bringing in reinforcements to attempt another Great Escape. Unfortunately, it wasn't to be. A dreadful run of form in the league meant that Birmingham would never escape from the relegation zone. A humiliating exit from the FA Cup at the hands of non-league Kidderminster Harriers put the seal on a catastrophic season and Birmingham were eventually relegated by goal difference.

Fry wasn't to be beaten though. Again, he bought and sold players at an astonishing rate, leading Jasper Carrott to comment that Fry seemed to be, "trying to tackle the city's unemployment problem single-handedly". He brought in a plethora of new names who would help guide the Blues to a triumphant and cathartic Division Two title with a successful trip to Wembley in the Auto Windscreens Shield bundled in as well. Birmingham's return to the second flight was low key and stable, but not the runaway success that David Sullivan and Karren Brady craved. At the end of the 1995/96 season, with Birmingham in 15th place, Fry was replaced by local hero Trevor Francis.

Fry reappeared at Peterborough the next season and promised to take the team out of the Third Division. He kept his word, but not the way he'd have preferred, and they were promptly relegated to the fourth amid a financial crisis that would later see Fry heading a consortium to take over the club. Peterborough were promoted through the play-offs three seasons later, but slipped back down to the basement in Fry's final season of management in 2004/05.

Without Fry, Southend barely won another game in the 1993/94 season. As Fry had feared, Peter Taylor took over but was unable to repeat his predecessor's success. After a handful of seasons struggling manfully in mid-table, they slipped down in 1996/97 and then on to the bottom flight the following year.

Vic Jobson died in 1999 with the club firmly back in the doldrums. Fry mourned his passing, telling the *Southend Echo* that though they did not part on good terms professionally they remained friends afterwards.

Throughout our conversation he was keen to impress that his own financial stability was the result of Jobson's advice and friendship. Before arriving at Southend, he didn't even have a pension. "I wouldn't have what I've got now if it hadn't been for Vic Jobson," he told me.

Now Director of Football at Peterborough, Barry Fry is confident of a new era of success at the club. Wealthy Irish property tycoon Darragh

MacAnthony has taken control behind the scenes and Darren, son of Sir Alex, Ferguson is in place as manager. Fry's years of struggle to keep the financial wolves from the club's door are mercifully over.

But will he be happy now to relax? Will he pop up somewhere else for one final hurrah as a manager? With Barry Fry, you just can't rule anything out.

Barry Fry's autobiography, *Big Fry*, is published by HarperCollins Willow.

2 ⚽ ESPEN BAARDSEN
I'm a Footballer, Get Me Out of Here (1997–2003)

The demands of Espen Baardsen's new career meant that pinning him down for lunch was always going to be difficult. Instead, he invited me over to his flat in Covent Garden, for a breakfast interview. I duly turned up at 9.30am, clutching a bag of donuts.

"Not for me, thanks," he smiled. "I've just finished at the gym."

Baardsen is six foot five and looks like he could tear telephone directories in half two at a time. If he says he doesn't want a donut, I'm not going to argue.

His flat is absolutely magnificent. Towering, bright white walls support a high ceiling that looks down on an impeccable assembly of lavish furniture, plasma screens and paintings. The kitchen looks like the set of a cookery show and I swear I can *hear* it gleaming when I play back the interview later that day.

We perch on stools in the kitchen and chat about his time at Tottenham and the chain of events that led him to turn his back on an industry most people would happily kill to be a part of.

Baardsen, despite his intimidating frame, is warm, hospitable and friendly. He thinks deeply about every answer he gives and has a tendency to stop speaking halfway through a sentence and then start again from a different, more articulate direction.

He was born to Norwegian parents, but brought up in northern California. A promising goalkeeper as a child, he was spotted by Tottenham and began travelling to London every summer holiday to train with the youth team, staying in contact with youth coach Pat Holland throughout the year. In 1995, he was signed to the club permanently by then-manager Gerry Francis.

When reserve goalkeeper Chris Day left the club in 1996, Baardsen was elevated to second choice goalkeeper and took his place on the substitutes bench. His career in professional football had begun.

My childhood hero and one of the men who had recommended me to Tottenham, Erik Thorsdvedt, warned me about English football when I first arrived at White Hart Lane. One day, he told me, he'd gone to pick up his goalkeeper gloves and found that Paul Gascoigne had pooped in them. He'd just slipped them on and there it was; a little dark surprise from Gazza.

English football is strange when you're from a different background. I'd been coming to Tottenham from America every summer since I was 14, playing with the first year apprentice boys and trying to prove myself, but my first full year there was still pretty darn difficult. It was quite a transition to come over from the US and try to get used to all the banter. In that first year I was one of only two foreigners in the dressing room. I was totally unproven, I hadn't come from another club where I had achieved anything and I was quite lucky to be cast on to the bench as second choice goalkeeper.

It was hard to get used to the sense of humour in the dressing room. I never had anything as grotesque as Erik's present from Gazza, it was more the verbal abuse. I would just shut up if they started giving me stick, but that never seemed to help. Justin

Edinburgh and Steven Carr could be quite vocal, but everyone had their turn in there and it took me a while to realise that no one respects you if you don't slap them back. Eventually I started to give as much shit as I was taking.

I made my debut at Anfield [in 1997], coming on as a substitute for Ian Walker at half-time. I had the Tottenham fans behind me and they were great, just shouting, "Yiddo! Yiddo! Yiddo!" over and over again! It's so different from reserve games. There you can hear everything. It's so quiet and you always get a small group of men trying to put you off, saying some truly horrible things. Here it was just a collective roar.

We were losing when I came on and at the end, well, we ended up losing by the same score. I guess that sort of counts as a clean sheet, doesn't it? I kept my place to meet Coventry the next game and I felt like I played well there too. I got more confident after that and I was happier in the dressing room.

Gerry Francis was my first boss at Spurs and he was very much the old school English manager. Training was all about the five-a-sides, which the players loved. Gerry was pretty tough on me, probably deservedly so, but he was the one to give me my chance and I wouldn't have made it without him. Leading up to that Liverpool match I hadn't really impressed that much and I was just holding on to that number two spot. I was kind of lucky that Alan Sugar [Chairman at the time] was too stingy to bring in anyone more experienced!

It didn't work out for Francis and after him we had David Pleat for a short while. He was proper old school! He'd be getting us bouncing up and down while we were stretching and you could see the physios recoiling in horror!

Christian Gross came in next [1997] and I felt sorry for him. He had great training sessions, but his poor English didn't help him at all. He couldn't pick up on what the players were saying to him, which meant people could talk shit about him and he wouldn't even realise. Gerry would have spotted that in about two seconds. He ran out of time in the end. He had an awful start to the season losing the first two games.

It wasn't awful for me though. After that second defeat, and with near-riots kicking off outside the stadium, I walked past Alan Sugar in the corridor. I got on OK with Alan, we used to discuss share prices every now and then in the dressing room.

"Alright, son?" he said. "You fancy playing on Saturday?"

"Yeah!" I said, thinking it was some kind of joke.

"Fine, you're in the team then."

I don't know what was happening, and I don't think he was actually picking the team, but it had obviously been discussed. I was recalled to the side and we won the third match against Everton, but then they fired Gross anyway.

We were all a bit surprised by the appointment of George Graham [1998], but he was a respected coach and he certainly solidified the defence. Unfortunately, he wasn't a fan of me and that obviously influences my view of him. I had some good games under him, notably a clean sheet against Arsenal, but I was a little too erratic. Anyway, a guy like George Graham was never going to have a 20-year-old goalkeeper, was he? I had a feeling with him that I was not only going to have to perform well, but I was going to have to be the most in-form goalkeeper in the Premier League if I wanted to keep my place.

Things got even worse for me when I spoke to a Norwegian journalist about renewing my contract and I said that I was going to see how things turned out. I don't know how this got translated, but it was a quick, harsh lesson in the wisdom of doing telephone interviews. The next weekend *The News of the World* had me on the back page saying, "Stick your contract, George!"

I don't know how I made the back page, I'm not that important! Anyway, as you can imagine, I got paraded in on Monday morning and George was so pissed off. He'd been on the phone to my agent, Rune Hague, first thing in the morning saying that he was going to fine me.

I said, "Look, it's not my fault!" The funny thing was that it seemed to do the trick. Two months later when I actually did sign the contract, Rune told me that my salary just kept going up because of the negotiating power. Maybe you have to really ruffle feathers in order for anything to happen. If you're the nice guy, I guess you just get taken advantage of.

In the end I left anyway [2000]. I had heard that Neil Sullivan was coming in, but I'd also heard that Watford wanted me. I was sad to leave Tottenham. It's a great club and the fans there were so good to me. I had a lot of memories, a lot of experiences, but in the end I wasn't playing enough matches.

Graham Taylor was the manager at Vicarage Road and he was good for me. There was no insecurity, he didn't need to tell me that I was his number one. Watford would never have spent that kind of money on a reserve goalkeeper. Remember, this was a little while before Vialli turned up and started spending like a drunken sailor.

We started the season really well, going on a long unbeaten run of 15 games. The atmosphere in the dressing room was much the same as it was at Spurs, though obviously the players weren't being paid anywhere near as much money.

It was at Watford that I first began to realise that perhaps football wasn't for me. As a footballer, the holiday period is the most miserable time of the year. You have games and training sessions non-stop, you're in a hotel on Christmas Day and New Year's Eve. You have no choice over when you take holidays or what you can do. It sounds silly, I know, but imagine not ever getting to spend Christmas with your family and having to go hurl yourself around a cold, wet muddy field instead.

I'd started to become attracted to the financial world when I was at Tottenham, just as a hobby, but it really came to fruition at Vicarage Road.

The biggest problem with football, and the thing that no one ever realises, is that you have so much time on your hands. You sit around waiting for training, waiting for games, you wait for team coaches and then sit around waiting on them. It's a ton of sitting around and waiting.

Rather than fill that time by playing cards, I wanted to fill it by reading things that I thought I'd need in the future. And that's what I did. I read financial books, financial newspapers, I educated myself and I became quite dedicated to it.

Naturally, it got a bit of a reaction from the players, but it wasn't that bad. I've said already how much ribbing there was in the dressing room anyway, so you can imagine what it was like once they saw a copy of the *Financial Times*. The thing was, they could see me reading it and take the piss for a while, but once they saw I was really serious about it, they quickly got bored.

I had my own website with Icons.com and I've since heard that the guys there were a bit shocked by my updates. Apparently all the other players were just talking about football and I was sending thousands of words of financial predictions. I tell you what though, I would be a billionaire if I'd have backed those tips! Man, I wish I was as accurate now as I was then!

I even did an Open University degree while I was at Watford. I just wanted to get a degree under my belt even though, to be honest, it's made absolutely no difference to my career now! It was difficult though, because with the OU you're not going to classes and you have to do it all on your own. After a while you feel like all the new information is bottling up inside and you want like-minded people to express these new feelings to. Sure as hell couldn't do that in the Watford dressing room though! I was still going out with the other players here and there, but I was starting to move in different circles. Whereas at Tottenham I'd hung around with Stefan Iverson a lot, now most of my friends were from outside of football.

At Vicarage Road, though, things were about to change dramatically. In came Gianluca Vialli [2001] and a whole host of new signings. We knew life under the former Chelsea boss was going to be pretty different when he started taking us to five star hotels for pre-season. With Graham Taylor it had been £20-a-night hostels, so this, from a player's point of view, was brilliant news.

But on the pitch, I had my doubts. I don't think he knew what was required for that division. We needed players who could thrive in the scrappy conditions and we weren't able to mesh properly when so many new faces came in.

Vialli didn't like to shout and scream like other managers. Usually he'd spend most of half-time trying to find somewhere to smoke! He was like a teenager, trying to have a cigarette without his parents knowing, so he usually ended up in some side-room.

It wasn't his fault that his arrival coincided with the sudden economic downturn in football. You have to stand in awe of those guys at the Football League who were dumb enough to sign a huge deal with OnDigital without realising they were a credit risk. That agreement should have been made with the companies behind it, not with the new firm. The guy who set that deal up ... well, he must have been an idiot.

The football teams had all signed a contract and been promised millions of pounds over the next few years. Naturally, they'd gone out and invested the money straightaway in new players. When OnDigital suddenly announced that no one was going to get paid, it destroyed every league club's long-term financial plans at a stroke. I knew that I'd be out the door soon afterwards. Vialli had dropped me before Christmas and I could see it coming. I was one of the best-paid players at the club and I wasn't getting in the team. That meant that I was under serious pressure to leave.

The problem was that I had two and a half years left on my fairly lucrative contract at that point. Because of the financial collapse, everyone was broke and I didn't stand a chance of getting a salary like that elsewhere. I sure as hell wasn't just going to give up on the best paid years of my career. I mean, would you? But the club was in dire straights and a new board came in and attempted to salvage things. I couldn't believe that anyone would have a chance of turning it around, but the new administration somehow managed to pull it off. One of the first things they did was to beg with the players to take a wage cut. We agreed and I think that kept the wolf from the door for a while.

Unfortunately, my time at the club ended in quite a bit of tension. The results had been poor and Vialli left to be replaced by Ray Lewington [2002]. By now, out of the team and out of love with the game, I'd stopped caring. I couldn't get enthused about another season of reserve team football and I came back overweight for pre-season, Ray wasn't happy, but he didn't bother working things out with me. He didn't want to build me up, he didn't want to see that perhaps I wasn't happy and that he might be able to get the best out of me with a different approach, he just wanted me out. The thing was that by that point, I was fine with it because I think that's what I wanted anyway.

It got a little bit silly in the end. We had a meeting and I said, "Look, I can show up to training every morning, kick the ball about a bit and not give a shit for two years or we can sort something out." In the end we reached a settlement and I left the club.

At that point I genuinely thought my career was over. I took some time out and started to think about doing some travelling, but then something happened to make me think again. I was on a ferry coming back from France, when I got a call from an agent telling me that Everton were interested in me [2003]. The thing was, I'd been in Calais stocking up on beer! Prime condition for a comeback! They had an injury crisis at Goodison Park and they wanted me in as cover for a month. They were so professional at Everton that I thought I should give it a go. I played just one game and ironically, it was against Tottenham!

I wasn't even supposed to play. I found out 15 minutes before kick off that Richard Wright's knee had gone again and suddenly there I was. I weighed more then than I do today, I hadn't played first team football for about 18 months and I was thrust back into the Premier League. We lost 4–3.

I didn't do too bad, none of the goals were my fault, but I wasn't in good shape and I failed to really influence the game in any way. I walked off that pitch and I knew that I wouldn't get another chance. I needed to put in a great performance that day if I wanted anyone to say, "Ah, Espen's still got it". It was make or break. The one good thing to come out of that day was the reaction of the Tottenham fans. I'll never forget how they gave me a standing ovation as I ran towards them for the second half and they'll never know how much it meant to me.

By now, I was sure that I'd never come back, but that agent rang again and said that Sheffield United were interested. I travelled up for a trial, but there was never a chance of it being the right move. I'd lived in London all the time and I knew I'd never be able to get used to Sheffield. Not wanting to knock the north of England, but one day up there was enough for me, I'm afraid.

I had one miserable morning in training and I went up to see Neil Warnock. He offered me a salary that was about 95 per cent less than I'd picked up in the past. It just wasn't going to happen. I went back to my hotel to think about it, but that didn't take long.

"Fuck this" I thought and I grabbed my bags and drove back to London. At one stage I just started crying; I thought, "I can't handle this". But that was it, I knew then what my future was going to involve and it wasn't going to be football.

I know that people will wonder why I didn't have a go at climbing back up the leagues, but that just seemed ridiculous to me. I knew I was going to have to start again at the bottom, working my way up on tiny wages. If I started something new, I could secure a career for the rest of my life. If I went back to football, I'd have to scrap around just to have to start again anyway when I was 35.

In football you just want to be successful or the rest of the career is pretty much rubbish. I'd played in the Premier League and I'd been to a World Cup with Norway. To be a top flight player is an awesome experience. You can't beat that; it's a fantastic career to have. To scrape by in football, though, is awful.

It was totally the right decision. I was 25 years old and I wasn't going back to earning miserable money. I'd saved almost all of my wages from the good times, I was financially secure and I had no intention of going back.

As soon as I'd made my mind up, I went travelling and what an incredible sense of freedom it was. Life was completely different. I didn't have the stress of games coming up, I didn't have journalists bothering me; it was great.

I spent three months driving round the US, I went to South America for a couple of months, a couple of months driving round Australia, onto New Zealand and then I had a few months in south-east Asia. I could never have done that as a footballer.

When I returned I started to look around for a new job. I was spending most of my time investing my own money and living on the returns. I invested in a financial firm where I came into contact with a guy called Hugh Hendry. I told him about my situation and we met up for coffee a couple of times to discuss my options. The idea of a former footballer becoming a financial analyst might seem daft, but you'd be surprised how open some people can be to ideas if they come from someone passionate.

Not long afterwards, Hugh quit his job and set up a new company, Eclectica. He contacted me and asked if I'd like to work for him. We started off slowly and it went from there.

My first day in an office was absolutely fine. I was safe in the knowledge that no one was going to poop in my gloves! It was good; it was different. The guys there are great and they made me feel welcome. Most of them know more about football than I do!

The biggest thing I miss is the buzz you get when you make a big save, or the feeling you have when the fans cheer your name or sing a song about you. No amount of money will ever replace that. I can make a deal here, make some money, you know, and that's all great but it doesn't compare to the feeling you get when you run towards a stand of people and they're all standing up and applauding you.

I still like football, but I'm so much happier doing what I'm doing now. I don't blame anyone else for what happened. Were there people who could have turned my career around? Yes. But that doesn't mean it was their fault. At the end of the day, it was down to me.

In the end, I'm actually extremely glad at the way it all turned out. There's a few people I'd like to see again though. I'm doing a bit of cable television now and I wouldn't mind getting in touch with Sir Alan Sugar now that he's a celebrity. I think I'd like to tell him that he was fired, I'd get a kick out of that!

Espen Baardsen quit professional football at the age of 25, telling his Icons website that his heart was no longer in it.

"I think it is fairly accurate to say that a footballer who is not passionate about football will not get much success or enjoyment out of the game," he wrote.

Watford's new board eventually turned the club around, risking the fans' fury by sacking the popular Ray Lewington in 2005, but then replacing him with Aidy Boothroyd. The Hornets were promoted to the Premier League through the play-offs at the end of the 2005/06 season and their one season in the limelight secured their short-term financial future.

After travelling the world for a year, Baardsen joined Hugh Hendry at Eclectica.

"We have £400 million under management, part of it is a hedge fund where we can invest in anything, the other money is in equity funds," he told me. "I'm involved mostly on the macro fund side, which means I do a lot of complicated, funky trades."

While he spends most of his time working for Eclectica, he also occasionally appears on satellite television as a financial expert.

"I find I'm much happier now," he said as I finished off the donuts. "It probably stems from the freedom to do whatever the heck I want in terms of choices in life. Now, more than before, I actually really enjoy what I'm doing.

"I think I can probably handle the pressure in finance better than I could in football. When things go wrong, you can deal with the problem without having thousands of supporters breathing down your neck. It's nice to have my life back and have the freedom to choose what I do and when I do it."

Espen Baardsen now works for the investment fund, Eclectica. You can find out more about them at www.eclectica-am.com.

3 ⚽ RON HARRIS
Playing Through the Pain (1970)

Perhaps I've just seen one too many British gangster films, but when I arrived at the Chelsea Village Hotel to meet Ron 'Chopper' Harris, I have to confess that I was absolutely terrified.

It had a little bit to do with the fact that Harris's menacing cockney accent brings back shivering recollections of Lenny McClean in *Lock Stock and Two Smoking Barrels*, but a lot more to do with his reputation, which goes so far ahead of him that it's usually kicked its way through the front door before he even arrives in the neighbourhood.

Ron Harris was born in Hackney in the East End of London in 1944 and, after joining the Chelsea youth team in 1959, made his debut for the senior Chelsea side in 1962. He quickly forged a reputation for tough, uncompromising defending, which is a polite way of saying that he scared the shit out of everyone he played against.

Thankfully, when I met him he was charm personified. Admittedly, he still looked like a ganglord, radiating the kind of dormant power that is only generated when really hard blokes wear a nice suit, but he was all smiles and eager to speak about his favourite day in football.

In 1967 Harris became the youngest captain ever to lead a team out in the FA Cup Final, but that record was the only accolade he took from the day. Chelsea were beaten 2–1 by Tottenham Hotspur. Three years later, he had a chance to make amends, but this time it would be against Leeds United. Don Revie's men had every bit as nasty a reputation as Harris and the resulting matches, particularly the replay, could be used by desperate parents as a way of scaring their misbehaving children.

Harris visibly glowed when recollecting the games, using his hands to illustrate exactly how he wrote himself into football infamy in the opening stages of the replay. When it comes to corporate glad-handing and entertainment, he is a consummate professional, but his first love will always be his time on the pitch. Harris is a firm believer that the 1960s and 70s were a golden age of football and his enthusiasm, not to mention that dormant power I was talking about, makes it difficult to argue with him.

You suspect that part of the reason he holds the memory of 1970 FA Cup Final so dear is that he wasn't even supposed to be able to take part in it.

I'll always look back on the 1970 FA Cup Final as the defining moment, the absolute highlight of my career. I know we won the European Cup Winners' Cup not long afterwards but this was back when winning the FA Cup still meant as much to a club as winning the league, you know?

Both Chelsea and Leeds had had very good seasons. They'd come second in the league and we'd come third, so there was a lot of excitement about the game. I've said to people since that we had a good team, but we had three truly exceptional players in our side. With Peter Osgood up front, Alan Hudson and Charlie Cook in the team we had every right to be confident. Mind you, Leeds had their stars too. They had Billy Bremner, Johnny Giles and Eddie Gray. We were evenly matched, two good teams.

They were similar to us in that they had a tough back four that could have a bit of a dig when they wanted to, to put it mildly. When a game got tough, they got tougher and they had a bit of a reputation for it. But then we had myself, John Dempsey, David Webb and Eddie McCreadie and we could look after ourselves. I suppose it was always going to get a bit physical, wasn't it?

Both sides respected each other though, and there was a rivalry that still continues today. The fans have got a real thing for this game and even if Leeds was to come down to Stamford Bridge and play us tomorrow, I reckon that the atmosphere would be as fierce now as it was back then.

I think they used to say up north that the southerners were a bit of a soft touch, but they soon got that rammed down their throats, didn't they? With Chelsea just being five minutes off the King's Road and with the swinging '60s just coming to an end, we got tarnished with all that soft stuff. Thing was, if a team did come down to Stamford Bridge thinking like that, they wouldn't think it for very long. There was nothing soft about our side.

Even our strikers had a bit about them. The likes of Peter Osgood and Ian Hutchison were more than a handful for any pair of central defenders. I'm sure that if you were to ask big Jack Charlton and Norman Hunter who the toughest players they had to mark were, Ossie and Hutch would be right up there. No one liked marking those two.

In the dressing room before the first game at Wembley, the spirit was good. I wasn't nervous beforehand, I was just grateful to be playing. Earlier that week I'd been told I had no chance of getting on the pitch at all. I'd been on one of my famous long runs a few weeks before and I'd pulled a muscle in my leg. In fact, up until the Thursday before the game, I could barely walk at all.

Dave Sexton, the Chelsea manager, came in on the Thursday and told me I was probably out. I was so desperate to play, but at that stage the only solution I was being offered was a trip to a faith healer.

Dave said to me, "Look, if you really want to take the gamble, we're quite happy to have you see a specialist on Harley Street for a cortisone injection."

Well, that was it; I was straight in the taxi! I wasn't going to miss an FA Cup Final at Wembley.

Now, I'm not ... how shall I say ... a person who is afraid of pain, but I've got to say, a cortisone injection is quite uncomfortable. It's a big thick needle and it numbs the whole area completely.

No, it wasn't pleasant, but when I got back to the training ground, I couldn't believe the difference. The jab had killed the pain completely and suddenly I could run again. After all that, I was finally able to lead Chelsea out on to that famous pitch.

Mind you, the old pitch wasn't looking very good that day at all. In fact, it was an absolute disgrace. They'd had the Horse of the Year show on it not long before the game and it was like a ploughed field. Can you imagine that happening nowadays? There'd be uproar.

Leeds' first goal just summed up how stupid and difficult it was to play on. Big Jack Charlton headed a ball down into the six-yard box and me and Eddie McCreadie both went for it. The ball came down, but it never come back up again. It just hit the deck and went under Eddie's leg as he lashed out where he thought it should be. We held our hands up, me and Eddie, and I suppose you could blame us if you want, but if that had been on a normal pitch, it would have been fine.

Then when we equalised, it was down to that pitch again. Peter Houseman drove a long shot in on goal and Gary Sprake, the Leeds keeper, went straight over it. Usually it would have bounced up off the grass, but not in this game.

I'd had another cortisone injection before the game, but I wasn't match fit at all. I hadn't trained for three weeks. The pitch was ankle deep in mud, the game was played at a frantic pace and I come off just before the final whistle. Believe in me, I was absolutely fucked.

They thought they'd won it when Mick Jones stuck home a rebound with six minutes to go, but we got ourselves out of jail right at the end. John Hollins whipped a cross in and Ian Hutchison nodded one in with two minutes left.

The good thing for us was that they were still involved in European competition and the replay was a few weeks later. That gave me all the time I needed to get over my injury.

Now, Leeds were by far the better side on the day at Wembley, but we went away confident that it would all be different in the replay. We didn't play well but we got ourselves back into it. They were a formidable team Leeds, but we honestly thought that if we could play badly and hold them, then come the replay we had a great chance of finishing them off.

The game was up at Old Trafford, which was obviously much easier for the Leeds fans to get to. I thought our fans might get outnumbered, but there were loads of them. They were absolutely fantastic as well. We needed them to get behind us and appreciated them so much that night.

There was nothing new in the team talk. Certainly we weren't under any orders to get physical with them or anything like that. We played almost exactly the same way we always did.

There was just one change. Eddie Gray had given David Webb the biggest chasing that I've ever seen anyone get in that first game. Webby had all kinds of problems with him. As soon as we got back in the dressing room after the first game, Dave Sexton come over and he said he were going to swap us around. I was going to go to right back and pick up Eddie Gray and Webby was going to move into the centre.

Everyone knows how that worked out for Eddie, don't they? You've probably seen the tape. It took me just five minutes to sort him and it was a proper knee cruncher. Bang. He didn't come near me for the rest of the game. As he went to turn, I come in from the side and that was it. He never caused me any problems after that. I've said to people since, as much as Webby got the accolades for getting the winning goal, I deserved a pat on the back for taking Gray out the game that early.

And you know what? I didn't even get booked. If you'd done that today, you'd get banned for life, wouldn't you?

I think that challenge set the tone for the game that most people describe as the most notorious FA Cup Final of all time. That David Ellery, the ex-referee, did a TV programme on it once. He sat there watching the video and afterwards he said there should have been about eight red cards. Different game back then, weren't it?

There were tackles flying about all over the place, punches being exchanged and then our goalkeeper, Peter Bonetti, got done. He was bundled into the net by one of their players and limped his way through the rest of the game. It meant he couldn't do much about Mick Jones' opener and there we were, 1–0 down.

Funny thing was, we didn't lose faith at all. Anyone will tell you, if you're chasing two goals with 20 minutes to go, then you're up against it. When you're only one down though, whatever opposition you're up against, you've always got a chance. If we got 11 supporters out of the ground to play the Chelsea first team tomorrow, even they'd have that one chance to score.

Well, we got our one chance alright, and what a good thing it was that it fell to Peter Osgood. There was a long cross into the box and he lost his marker and got on the end of it with a fantastic diving header. It was such a brave header, typical of the man. I've said to people before, he was the most gifted individual I ever played with at Chelsea. He was big, but his first touch was terrific and he had a bit of muscle as well. He wasn't afraid to put himself about a bit.

The game went to extra-time again and then we got a throw, in between the halfway line and penalty area. Ian Hutchison hurled it so far it was more like a cross. David Harvey, the Leeds keeper, come out, but he didn't get there in time. The ball got flicked on and there was Webby at the far post to bundle it in.

Well, that was that, wasn't it? We didn't show any nerves at all, we just knuckled down and held on. I think Eddie Gray had a shot that went 40 yards over the bar and we sensed then that it was going be our day. Their heads had gone down after the equaliser, but when Webby stuck it in, they was finished.

The celebrations were amazing. We had a great bunch of lads at Chelsea and if you saw the state of the England cricket team when they won the Ashes, you'll have an idea of what happened to us that night.

We had a bit of the old champagne in the dressing room, having a bit of a swig in the bath and singing, it was great. I can remember going back to the hotel with the directors and everything, having a meal and then we went up town.

I don't know how long we were out, but we had to get the first train up to the Lord Mayor's place so we could stand about with the trophy. There were a lot of hangovers that day. We had some big drinkers in that team, but even the quiet ones had a few drinks that night!

I've said to people since that all those blokes, even the fringe players, were fantastic. I was privileged to have captained such a great bunch of lads. If you'd have come in and said your son was in hospital, we would have had a word and I would guarantee you that you'd get at least six of our lads going in and saying hello.

But, like I say, it was a different ball game back then. We had a club policy of staying in a hotel on a Friday night, home or away, and if we were in town, we'd go watch the dogs at Wimbledon. As long as you was back in the hotel by 10pm, no one said a word. They couldn't do that now.

Nowadays you're told what to do, what to eat and where to eat. They're trained athletes now, aren't they? We used to have a pre-match meal, now this is at 12 o'clock remember, three hours before kick off, and it would be steak; steak with tea, toast and rice pudding as a sweet. Occasionally someone would have a bright idea and give you a Mars bar before the game to perk you up. That's as technical as it got.

It's like that Cup Final. Everyone laughs at it now and calls it the most violent game of all time, but that's how it was back then. I'm not being disrespectful to today's generation, but it's a non-contact sport now.

But before people get upset, you have a look at what you get in the modern game. We might have weighed in with some heavy tackles, but at least no one ran 40 yards to remonstrate with the ref afterwards. No one was jumping up and down waving pretend red cards, what's that about? That's a habit that's right out of order. No one made a meal of their injuries either, rolling about on the floor and all that. They just dusted themselves down and got on with it.

Years ago, when you played in these European competitions, the last thing the manager used to tell you before you went down the tunnel was to be careful around the box. "You know what they're like," they'd say. Everyone does it now. There's not a week goes by without someone falling over to try and get someone sent off, and I think that's a shame. When you watch football, you want to see a proper game, but they do go down a bit easy these days, don't they?

I tell you what, it would do some players a lot of good to go and watch a rugby game and see how what goes on there. People just get up and accept the referee's decision and they definitely don't run 40 yards to try and get a fellow professional sent off.

How would I fare in today's game? Well, I think I'd do alright. I'd like to think that I had good positioning, marking and concentration and, touch wood, I think I'd do quite well. With regard to the tackles though, it would most probably be a bit more difficult!

That said, I like to think there was more to my game than just kicking. I do a lot of after-dinner speaking now and I always get these people coming up to me saying, "My dad told me that all you used to do was fucking kick people," but I tell you what, I've played more games for Chelsea than anyone else. I played under seven managers and I was captain for half the 19 years I was at the club. I must have been a bit more than just someone who fucking kicked people, mustn't I? I hope so anyway.

You know, you look back at games like this one and I think, if you spoke to old football fans, they'd say it was more exciting in our day than it is now.

Football can be like a game of chess these days. Did you see that Cup Final in 2007, Chelsea against Manchester United? I was there, sitting next to Frank McLintock and I said, "Frank, if this had been in our day, they'd have booed us off!" They'd have done the slow handclap after 20 minutes.

People say that they're all athletes now and it's a better, quicker game, but I'm telling you, back in our day you had people like Ozzy, Besty, Denis Law and that, loads of real good players playing on pitches what looked like shit-heaps. We played on frost, in snow, in torrential downpours, the only thing what stopped us was fog.

When you look at the pitches today, it's unbelievable. Even I'd have good control on them! You can't compare the current Chelsea side with our one, because it's a totally different sport. I'm not saying today's generation couldn't do it, but I wouldn't mind seeing them having to go up to Anfield on a cold night and have Tommy Smith breathing down their arse!

Yeah, that Cup Final was an amazing moment. The only unfortunate part was that it had to be at Old Trafford. I'm not being disrespectful to Manchester United, it's a fantastic stadium, but I'd have preferred to play at Wembley again. Not getting the opportunity to walk up those steps and pick up the trophy there takes the gloss off a little. I'd have liked to have walked up those steps, you know?

Ron Harris stayed at Chelsea until 1980, playing an extraordinary 795 competitive games for the club. He then spent three years as a player-coach for Brentford and was tempted into a short spell as player-manager of Aldershot when friends of his took over the club.

"Within six months though, the old board came back again and that was it," he said. "I only took it on 'cos they was friends of mine."

He wasn't tempted to return to management at all. "When you leave Brentford in the Third Division, where do you go from there?" he asked. "You look at managers at that level and if it's not working out for them after 18 months, they get the boot. Bit too precarious, isn't it?"

Harris now works on the hospitality team at Chelsea, and, after a long period where he went unrecognised at the club, finally has a VIP suite in the stadium named after him.

"They had an entrance named after Nigel Spackman but nothing named after me," he laughed. "Fair play to Nigel, he was a decent player, but he was only here five minutes!"

He, and a number of the Chelsea old guard, were frozen out by the former chairman Ken Bates in the '80s and '90s. When Roman Abramovich took over, he met Harris and spoke with him through a translator for an hour about the history of the club. Now, the former skipper is in attendance for almost every home game, immaculate in his suit and primed for meeting and greeting.

I met Harris on the day of the Champions League match with Rosenborg, the game that saw the end of Jose Mourinho's reign, and we discussed the frenzied media reports. He was, of course, far too clever to say anything that might reflect badly on Chelsea, but also pointedly refused to answer any questions about Mourinho's prospects of staying in charge. Forty-eight hours later and with Mourinho gone, he was being interviewed by Sky Sports News, who were desperately trying to stir up hysterical reactions from anyone concerned with the club. His was the only sound-bite not to be repeated throughout the day, probably because it was the only sound-bite with any perspective.

"Chelsea were here before Mourinho," he said solemnly, "and they'll be here after Mourinho. Whatever else happens, there'll always be a Chelsea."

Ron Harris's autobiography, *Chopper – A Chelsea Legend*, is published by Big Blue Tube.

4 ● PETER SHILTON
One Final Chance of Glory (1990)

To speak to him, you wouldn't guess that Peter Shilton had represented his country more times than any other English footballer. I've interviewed players from this generation who haven't played as many *league* games as he has internationals and yet they carry the demeanour and arrogance of a multiple World Cup winner. But Shilton doesn't do arrogant. He's modest about his achievements when he shouldn't have to be and speaks in a very straightforward manner about a period for the England team that was anything but.

Warm, but stoic in a very British way, he keeps his guard up throughout our conversations, only letting his defences slip when describing the final moments of the 1990 World Cup and his Achilles heel, "that goal" by Diego Maradona in 1986. As soon as he realises, he pauses and then continues with a stiffer upper lip.

"What can you say about Peter Shilton? Peter Shilton is Peter Shilton and he has been since the year dot," said Bobby Robson once, summing both of them up rather nicely. He was born in 1949 and began his playing career in the year that England won the World Cup. Astonishingly, not only was he still playing 24 years later but he was the goalkeeper to take them as close as they've ever been since.

His club career peaked in the late 1970s at Brian Clough's

Nottingham Forest where he won two European Cups and the 1978 Player of the Year award. Though he was a non-playing member of the squad in 1970, his first active World Cup was in 1982, where England were knocked out in the second group stage.

In 1986, England reached the last eight before being eliminated single-handedly by Diego Maradona and I mean that quite literally.

By 1990, Shilton was with Derby County and he was still wearing the number one shirt for his country. He'd picked up his 100th cap during the dismal European Championships of 1988, but this was to be his final chance for international glory.

As players, we were very excited when we set out for the 1990 World Cup in Italy. After a disappointing European Championships, we wanted to go out and prove ourselves again, but the press didn't think we had a chance and they absolutely slaughtered us.

I remember them really having a go at Bobby Robson before the tournament, not just about football, but for personal reasons as well. There was one article in particular that the players really got annoyed about because it was done in such a distasteful way and, after that, there was a lot of animosity to the newspapers. It wasn't so much the football writers, just the editors back home pulling the strings.

In a way, it might have helped us though. In the face of all that criticism, we rallied around the manager and everyone pulled together. We were out in Sardinia, training hard in the heat and doing our best to stay positive. Bobby was great though. He didn't let it get to him and he organised things so well that no one had time to dwell on it.

Bobby was a terrific football manager. He was organised, clever and enthusiastic and he always wanted the game to be played in the right way. Mind you, as everyone in football knows, he also had a few moments where his mind would go a bit blank!

There's quite a few stories about him, but they're all with the greatest respect because he was well loved by his players. No one ever doubted his abilities; it was just that he was a bit forgetful! There was one instance where we were having a team meeting and Bobby was putting a diagram on the board of our opposition with little magnetic counters for how they'd line up. This was one of Bobby's greatest strengths; he was terrific tactically. He was going on and on about the space on the right-hand side of their defence. "We've got to get down the left, lads," he was saying. "We've got to get up there and whip in those crosses because that's where they're at their weakest! This is where we can win the game, no problems!"

Don Howe suddenly interrupted and said, "Erm ... boss? I think we'd have more of a problem if you put their right-back on the board."

The players had already noticed and were trying desperately not to laugh, but that was typical Bobby, he'd just get so involved in it all. But that was all great for team spirit!

I was 40 years old when the World Cup kicked off, but, to be fair, I didn't actually consider it to be my last tournament. I felt as though I was still at a very high level. I mean, I carried on professionally after the World Cup for some time.

Someone close to Graham Taylor, the incoming England manager, had indicated to me that he would be interested in my carrying on as the number one and it was someone quite reliable, so I started that tournament with an open mind about my future. After all, the European Championships were only two years away. But that was all in the future, for that moment I just wanted to concentrate on playing.

Our first game was against Ireland, who had humiliated us in the Euros two years before. It was one of the strangest feelings I've ever had in a World Cup, that game. You build yourself up to play in a big global summer tournament and then you get there to bad weather, an old-fashioned stadium and a team full of opponents you've been playing against all season. I felt like I was playing a league match!

It wasn't the best game, either. Ireland played to their strengths, kicking into the channels and hitting it long to Cascarino and we both came off at the end thinking that the 1–1 draw wasn't a bad result at all. It was actually a good result when we found out that Holland had drawn with Egypt. The one thing you don't want to do in a World Cup is get beat in your first game, so that point got us moving.

I can't remember having a lot to do against Holland in the next one. I thought the Dutch were very disappointing. Having said that, I thought we played quite well and seemed to be a little bit more up for it. The players felt better that night, it seemed more like a typical World Cup game and I think we felt we should have won it, especially after having a goal disallowed. But a goalless draw was absolutely fine. It set us up nicely to play Egypt in the final match.

Egypt was a terrible game for a goalkeeper. You have everything to lose against a team like them. Before the match you think, "Terrific, we've got to beat Egypt to go through". Our attitude was that if we couldn't do that, we didn't deserve to go through.

As it turned out it was an awful game. We won 1–0, but even though they didn't press us we were on edge all the way through. At 1–0, anything can happen. They had a great chance when their fella had a clear shot from ten yards and he mis-hit it. I got down sharp and saved it, but I shouldn't have even been able to see it. I often think, you know, if that had gone in we could have been out of the

World Cup. One mistake, one slip, one goal and we'd have been going home in shame.

We hadn't killed anyone off in the group stage and that was a concern. However, even though we weren't playing at our best, we were still getting results. We were in touch with people back home, however, and we were well aware of what was being said in the newspapers. We knew there was some heavy criticism of our performances and we didn't like it.

We had Belgium in the second round and for a long time it seemed that it was going to penalties. It was a great game to play in; they played really well. They even hit the post at one point, but I knew I had it covered. Then Gascoigne played that high lofted ball into the box and Platty put it in the net with seconds to go. What a moment! At the end, big Terry Butcher was celebrating the way Terry does and Gazza came running up ... it was brilliant, just brilliant. You couldn't describe it. It was the perfect time to score, Belgium had no way of getting back into the game and it was a really exciting moment. Platty was obviously pleased because that goal made his career! All of a sudden, you know, it finally felt like a World Cup.

After the Belgium game the players decided to boycott the press. We felt like we'd had no support from them at all. We had such a tight unit together and we were so angry about those attacks on Bobby that we had to stand up for ourselves. It was just a constant assault, anything they could do to get at our players. Something happened with Gazza on a day out, I think he'd had a few drinks or something, and it was all over the papers that he'd let his country down!

Everybody knew Gazza and what Gazza was like. We all knew that he could be a match winner and we all knew he was a terrific player. He could do everything on his day. He could go past people, he was a dribbling midfielder and he had strength, passing and vision. Oh, and he could weigh in with a goal or two as well! We knew his capabilities and we knew he could be a bit of a pain in the backside on occasions. He could be his own worst enemy sometimes, but you couldn't help liking him.

Anyway, after that Belgium game, we all decided to make a stand. When you're putting yourself out to talk to the same journalists who've been slagging you in the papers and you're giving them quotes and helping them do their jobs, sometimes, you've just got to say, "Hold on a minute. Go find your own headlines". Everybody accepts criticism and everybody realises that things are going to be written, but there's a difference between that and being nasty. Sometimes, enough is enough.

We had to play Cameroon in the quarter-finals. This was a game that the rest of the world wanted to see us lose and if it had been anyone else playing them, I'd have wanted the African side to win as well! They'd beaten Argentina in the first game and the world was falling in love with them. But from our point of view, there was no time for the romance of the cup. There was a semi-final place on offer and we were taking it very seriously. We knew what to expect. Bobby had done his homework.

"Don't underestimate them!" he told us. "They are a good team. They've got a lot of ability."

The press thought it would be a walkover, but we didn't and we were right. It was a really tough match. They sliced us open early on and had a one-on-one in the first couple of minutes. That was it; it was definitely game-on then. Platty scored first and settled the nerves a bit, but then it all went wrong. They got an equaliser in the second half when Gazza hacked down one of their players. 1–1.

Moments later and they're one-on-one again and suddenly we were losing. When the game kicked off again I felt sick. My stomach was sinking. I thought, "Christ, we're going out. We're actually going out."

In the end, I think the occasion got to Cameroon a bit. I think they suddenly realised that they were on the verge of a semi-final and they lost their heads. They couldn't handle it. Giving away two penalties in the closing stages certainly supports that. Gary Lineker was given the responsibility and I had great confidence in him. I used to room with Gary and I knew him very well. I was sure that he wouldn't bottle it, no matter how intense the pressure. I was OK watching him put the first one away to make it 2–2, but the second one in extra time was almost too much to bear.

It's always harder to take a second penalty in the same match. The goalkeeper knows what your preferred option is and psychologically, he's got the upper hand. Later that night, Gary confessed to me that he really didn't know what to do when he stepped up to take it. He'd been coached well though, by George Dewis at Leicester, and he'd been taught to just concentrate on hitting the target. I know it sounds silly and basic, but so many strikers concentrate on putting it in the corners and end up missing the entire goal. You've got to work the keeper. Gary just wanted to get it on target, make a good connection and then see what happened.

He drove it straight down the middle of the goal, right down the keeper's throat. Fortunately, the Cameroonian goalkeeper decided to gamble and he'd thrown himself to the side as early as he could. The ball passed right through where he'd been standing. If he'd have just stood still ... well, we had that bit of luck, didn't we?

After that game, I got caught up in all the excitement. We'd come through the group without ever playing that well. We'd got to the semi-finals in extra time in both games and the little things were going our way. Surely, this was our year?

By now, I'd decided that this was going to be my final tournament as an England player. With Bobby leaving as well, it felt like the right decision at the right time. I'd thought long and hard about it and I had a chat with him and told him my decision. He asked me if I was certain and I was. Something in my mind was saying to me, "It's time". Physically I felt like I was on top of my game, but mentally, I wanted to finish on a good note.

The press had changed completely by then, of course. Surprise, surprise, eh? You realise then that they either go one way or the other – they're never balanced when it comes to England. Before the semi-final against Germany, Bobby was, if anything, more confident than he'd ever been before. We all were, really. We all knew that we were playing well, we were in the last four and we'd done ourselves proud. We were up for it. But when we got out there, we conceded first and it was a horrible goal. It was a fluke. It was unlucky and you can't say any more than that.

I actually felt that I reacted very quickly to it. The ball was knocked square from a free-kick and it was basically a clear shot on goal from 20 yards out. I got my angles right, but Paul Parker's tried to break his neck to block it and he gets there and it hits him on the shin. I thought I reacted quickly, but in the end it was pure bad luck. It didn't hit the bar; it didn't drop a few inches beneath the bar where I could tip it over. It just dropped where I couldn't get it.

I remember thinking then, sat there in the goal, I remember thinking, "I can't believe that that's happened. I don't want that to be the moment that costs us the World Cup."

I had a lot of time in that second half to reflect upon the fact that a freakish goal could be my final memory in an England shirt. When Gary Lineker scored in the last ten minutes I could have run up the field and kissed him on the lips! I really could! "Good old Links!" I thought. "We're back in the match!" That was the most relieved I've ever been in a game of football.

I know what it's like with bad luck in a football match. I had it with that Maradona goal in 1986. I'm getting the ball and he cheats and the referee doesn't see it. I made the right decision that day, I was going to get that ball ... but you rely on the referee, don't you? Sometimes things happen that you just can't control. It was a great game and I really enjoyed being in it. We were playing as well that night as we had in the entire tournament. I made a few good saves, one really good one from Klinsmann, and the game was well poised.

I have to be honest, I didn't see much of what happened with Gascoigne. I was so focused on which way the match was going to go. The whole incident was down the other end of the pitch, but even with that in mind, it was obvious what had happened. He'd done one of his lunging tackles and then realised that he was suspended for the final game. It was typical of him that he was so wound up that his emotions overcame him. It's not very often you see someone cry on a pitch. I can understand why it affected so many people, but that was him. He wasn't an ordinary footballer.

We should have sealed it in extra time. Chris Waddle had a chance to score and I actually thought it was heading in. Unfortunately it just cannoned off the post and back out again. That was the defining moment of the match for me; that was the line between success and failure.

And then it was penalties and when you get there you're just hoping for a bit of luck. There's different ways of thinking about them but as goalkeeper you always either guess right or you don't, don't you? You don't feel the pressure so much, you just focus on trying to stop them. I never wanted to move too early because so many penalties get scuffed down the middle, but every German penalty was struck perfectly. Quick, hard and in the corners, I had no chance with any of them.

Bodo Illgner had the luck. Poor Stuart Pearce did drive his down the centre and Illgner nearly dived straight past it, but it hit him on the knee and came back out again. That's the bit of luck you need in a penalty shootout.

When Chris Waddle stepped up, I still thought we'd be alright. All you can do is just stand there and stare at it, wanting to see the net ripple. When he ballooned it over the bar everything just stopped. In an instant, you realise you're out of the World Cup. It's gone forever. It was a terrible feeling. We walked off the pitch and out of the tournament.

But our misery wasn't complete. Me and Pearcie got pulled in for a routine drugs test and in that heat, with that dehydration, we were going to be there for a long time. We couldn't go back to the dressing room, we couldn't sit with our team-mates, we couldn't listen to our manager, we just had to sit in this small room with two of the German players trying to pee into a bottle.

To be fair, the Germans were OK about it all. We were gutted and they knew it, but the game was over. We didn't talk about it at all. We just got on with it.

When we finally produced the samples, the stadium was practically empty and the rest of the team had gone. Pearcie and I had to go back to the hotel on our own. I can't even remember what happened after that. It was all very disappointing.

It could have gone either way, but for the width of a post, but it didn't, did it? We knew that we'd given it everything, but there's a fine line between success and failure.

Regrets? No, I don't think so. There's a lot that I can look back on with pride. I think my record for England in terms of games played and goals conceded is something I'm very proud of and I'm just happy to have been part of the most successful England team to play in a World Cup overseas.

Peter Shilton played his last game for England in the Third/Fourth Place play-off against the host nation Italy. In a game that no one ever wants to take part in, the hosts were victorious, 2–1. England didn't go home empty-handed though, they were the eventual winners of the Fair Play Trophy.

The tournament and, in particular, Paul Gascoigne's tears, re-ignited the game's appeal in England. With dwindling attendances, decrepit stadiums and rampant hooliganism, football had been a dirty word in the 1980s, but this strange cocktail of tension, patriotism and emotional vulnerability brought thousands of new football fans flocking. Valiant failure has always been the opiate of the English and Bobby Robson's squad delivered that in abundance.

Robson left England after the tournament to take the PSV Eindhoven job. His success there led to further employment at Sporting Lisbon, Porto and then, magnificently, at Barcelona. He returned to England in 1999 to revive his boyhood team, Newcastle, where he stayed until he was cruelly sacked after a poor start to the 2004/05 season.

Shilton stayed with Derby until 1992 when he was appointed as the manager of Plymouth Argyle where he stayed until 1995. He returned to action after Argyle, joining a number of teams of goalkeeping cover including West Ham. In 1996, he signed for Leyton Orient and in front of the TV cameras played his 1,000th game against Brighton and Hove Albion.

Peter Shilton's autobiography, *The Autobiography*, is published by Orion. Peter is now an after-dinner speaker with Champions plc who can be contacted on 08453 313031.

5 ● DAVID ICKE
A Win Would Be Nice (1971)

When I mentioned to my friends that my next interviewee was David Icke, there was a consistent and predictable response. It's fair to say that the general public has some fairly entrenched preconceptions of who David Icke is and what he does. Basically, they think he's crackers and that he spends his days hiding behind the settee from a race of superior lizard-men.

This, I'm afraid to report, is not the case. Icke was kind enough to meet me at Ryde Docks where I arrived on the Isle of Wight and drive me to a small Italian restaurant in town for our lunch. His trademark grey hair has long since turned ghostly white and he's feeling the after-effects of a nasty bug, but I sense that he's actually looking forward to the interview. It must be the first time in 20 years that a journalist has approached him without wanting to talk about Wogan, purple shellsuits or the secret reptilian elite.

Icke is fascinating company. He is as passionate about football as he is about everything else in his life and at times during our meeting he argued fiercely against the sins of the modern game. With knowledge drawn from a career as both a professional footballer and a sports broadcaster, he knows what he's talking about.

He hates the fact that young academy players are treated so badly, despises the pursuit of money above glory and loathes the negative tactics of so many Premier League teams. In fact, it's just like discussing football with anyone else over the age of 35, except that it comes with so much righteous indignation that it would make an angry teenage political activist doubt their own commitment.

There are inevitably times when our conversation wanders into more flammable subjects and his renegade views certainly aren't for everyone. The interesting thing is that they're not actually that dissimilar from your average *Guardian* reader. Hate the war in Iraq? Check! Feeling disenfranchised from politics? Check! Think that George W. Bush is heavily influenced by big business interests? Check! Think that it's the fault of a shadowy, possibly alien, organisation who have influenced every aspect of humanity since the dark ages? Ah ...

Icke's only problem is that he takes every issue to a conclusion far beyond the limits of acceptability for the masses. Icke would say that that's their problem, not his, and with millions of book sales under his belt, he'd have a point. He might even be right about the conspiracies, I really don't know.

What I do know is that he is a friendly, accommodating chap with a long background in football, and he really doesn't deserve to be pilloried so mercilessly. A highly rated goalkeeper in the late 1960s, he was tipped for big things, but he suffered appalling luck when he picked up a persistent knee injury. His career in professional football was over before it had begun, but a stint in non-league football still beckoned. This time he would be in the hands of one of the finest footballers ever to play the game.

My professional football career started when I was signed by Coventry City at 15, but it didn't get much further than that sadly. A knee injury that turned into a lifetime of arthritis did for me, but not before I got to play for one of the greatest names in the history of football.

I started off playing for Leicester schoolboys in the '60s and I could have stayed there, but with Gordon Banks in the first team and Peter Shilton in the reserves, it's fair to say that my chances looked limited! Ironically, if I had have signed for them, by the time I would have been in contention for first team football, they'd both have gone anyway.

There were other clubs I could have had trials with, but my father always had this thing about Coventry City. At the time they were managed by Jimmy Hill. They'd come up from the Third Division and were running away with the Second, happily preparing for life in what is now the Premier League. My father was very impressed and he said, "I want you to go and have a trial for them." Now, they'd never seen me play so he had to write to them and get it all arranged. I turned up and it was such a bloody shambles, this trial, I was fed up with it straightaway. It must have helped me focus though because they signed me and four days later I was training with the first team.

Contrary to his TV persona, Jimmy Hill was actually quite distant from anything and anyone except the first team. But he did write a letter to my father, I've got it still somewhere, saying that one of his priorities had been to sign a first class youth goalkeeper. There was a lot of emphasis on youth at Coventry and we had a really good young team there.

They were a brilliant group of players who came together back then, actually. We got to the final of the FA Youth Cup against Spurs in 1969 and had to play four games before it was settled. Graeme Souness was playing for Spurs and, it's funny, he was exactly the same then as he is now. It was extraordinary; 16 years old and he was so full of himself, so aggressive and so nasty. Definitely not the kind of guy you'd like to go for a pint with. We lost the first leg 0–1 and he scored the winner. Then we won the second leg and he was booked. The third game was 2–2 and he was sent off and then in the final replay at White Hart Lane he scored the winner. That sums him up really.

I'm not surprised he's had problems as a manager though. When you're the boss you have to manage personalities and he must have struggled there. Some players respond to an arm on the shoulder and some respond to a rollicking, but if you get it wrong you're in serious trouble.

Anyway, Coventry surprised everyone by going up, staying up and then establishing themselves in the top flight for over thirty years. Of course, Jimmy Hill had quit by the time the club had started their season in Division One. There were rumours that he didn't think the squad was strong enough to survive and he chose to join ITV in a very different role. He was replaced by Noel Cantwell who was a lovely guy. His contribution to Coventry City should never be underestimated.

Unfortunately, I didn't get to play much of a part in this story. At the end of my first season at the club I got a knee injury. It didn't sort itself out properly and turned out to be the start of the arthritis. At the age of 19 I was told by a doctor that if I continued to train every day and play professional football, I'd have to spend the rest of my life in a wheelchair. I'd been marked out as a quality goalkeeper for the future, but now that future was completely up in the air.

The doctor, and I still remember this, he gave me this huge tin of painkillers and told me to take three a day for the rest of my life. If I'd have done that, I wouldn't be here now and I wouldn't have been here for a long time. Thank God that, even at 19, I knew what a stupid move that would be. I looked at those pills and I thought,

Barry Fry – one of the game's quiet, retiring types – in the dugout at Underhill in 1992. Fry dragged Barnet kicking and screaming into the Football League, but left in 1993 to perform similar miracles with Southend United.

Espen Baardsen makes a point during a pre-season friendly with Tottenham. This photo was taken in 1997 and, just a few years later, Baardsen would quit professional football to follow his dream of working in the financial sector.

Chopper Harris lifts the FA Cup after an epic encounter with Leeds United in 1970.
Can you see those perspiration marks? These were the halcyon days when you
could tell how much a player cared by his sweat patches. Mmmm...musky.

Peter Shilton laughed as his memorabilia cupboard collapsed on top
of him. No, not really. This is Shilts with 109 caps, taken in 1989
when he surpassed Bobby Moore's record. He went on to win 125.

David Icke, shortly before being asked to run off his arthritis. Icke's promising career was cut short by a knee injury and so, in 1971, he went semi-pro with John Charles' Hereford.

She may have lived her life like a candle in the wind but, when the rain came in, Princess Diana could always turn to Nigel Spackman who, in his tiny shorts and swanky sweatband before the 1988 FA Cup Final, represented all that was beautiful about the 1980s.

"You must be fucking joking." I'd rather be in pain and still have my stomach, thank you very much.

So, I left Coventry and I didn't have a clue what to do with myself. One of the club's directors, John Campkin, he owned a travel agent that later got taken over by Lunn Poly. He offered me a job working with him while I figured out what I wanted to do. Of course, I was the worst travel agent in the world; my heart wasn't in it at all. But it did come in handy. You see, Campkin knew John Charles, then the manager of non-league Hereford, and he tipped him off that I'd had to quit professional football.

Charles called me up and said, "I hear you've left Coventry, why don't you come and play for us?"

Now, getting a call from John Charles then was a little bit like getting a call from David Beckham or Gary Lineker now. Charles was the first British player to go to a foreign league and make a success of it. He'd been outstanding at Leeds United and had caught the attention of Juventus. They still rate him as one of the best players ever to wear those black and white shirts, you know? He could play as a centre-back, or as a centre-forward, but he was absolutely world class in either position. They called him the "gentle giant" in Italy because, unlike some players, he never used his huge frame to hurt anyone. He was a gentleman.

So, he's on the phone to me and he said, "Why don't you come down and play for us? It's semi-professional, so you only have to train once a week and we'll make sure that you don't have to do any running or anything that could affect your injury."

He was in his 40s at the time and he used to work with me a little bit on the training pitch. One of the things he'd do was he'd give me a load of balls and then I'd throw them up to him, so he could try and head them past me. The thing with John was, he'd do it from about

20 yards away. You'd throw these balls up and blam! They'd be coming back at you like bullets. It was incredible. You just thought, "Jesus Christ, what was this guy like when he was in his prime?"

John didn't do that much training though. Mainly, it was orchestrated by a guy called Peter Issacs who was a former Hereford goalkeeper himself. Peter was one of these survivor people who, no matter what changes took place in management, he was always there.

When I first arrived at the club, as I say, I'd agreed with John that I wouldn't do anything overly physical, so when Issacs came in and announced that the training session was going to be almost all running, I protested. I told him about the agreement I had in place with the manager.

He said, "What have you got?"

I said, "Rheumatoid arthritis."

He said, "Arthritis, eh? Well, come on then, lad, let's run it off!"

I never really got on with him after that.

John Charles was one of the nicest people I've ever met in my life, but it was quite clear that he wasn't going to be cut out for a career in football management.

I remember we had this one game and he was standing there at the dressing room door, waiting for us to go out there. It was all quiet in the dressing room and the only noise was a few nervous players impatiently bouncing balls up and down. We needed a pre-match speech.

"Right lads," said John loudly. "We've got to win tonight."

Everyone nodded and clattered their studs on the floor. There was a long pause.

"Well..." shrugged John. "We've not *got* to win, have we?"

The balls stopped bouncing.

"I mean ... it would be nice though, wouldn't it?"

And that was it! Not quite Winston Churchill, was it?! Oh, he tried to be a boss, he really did, but his heart just wasn't in it. He was such a gentle man and there was no way that he could do the bollockings. He didn't make decisions, he would stick with people that he shouldn't have been stuck with because he didn't want to hurt them and you know, just generally, he was indecisive. On one level, on a personal level, everyone loved him, but on another, people wanted some organisation, some decisiveness. In the end, that's why he went, I think.

Hereford was owned by this carpet salesman called Frank Miles. I think he got John in just to get bums on seats, because it seemed that it was him picking the team sometimes. I don't think John liked it very much at all and it was a partnership doomed to failure. Plus, Chairman Miles, as he was known in the dressing room, had the patience of Genghis Khan when it came to results. John was eventually sacked six months after I arrived and replaced by Colin Addison. You couldn't have got a more different character. Addison wouldn't take any interference from the chairman and he certainly wasn't the tender boss that John had been! After being sacked, John went to manage Merthyr Tydfil. For some reason, Hereford were allowed to play in the Welsh Cup in those days. The Welsh Cup was basically Cardiff's annual ticket into Europe, but we always gave it a go as well.

In one of those funny little coincidences that football throws up, we drew Merthyr and John Charles was playing. That night the ground was absolutely packed and the atmosphere was incredible. Every time the ball went anywhere near him, there was an almighty roar. We drew 0–0 and I managed to save one from him, to my left if I remember. He was way over 40 by this point, but he was still up there, battling away and trying to put one past his old goalkeeper.

I learnt a lot from working with John Charles, but most importantly I learnt that you can't be a nice guy all the time and be a successful manager, just like Souness couldn't be a nasty guy all the time. You have to know how to balance it. You have these clichés, like there's no room for sentiment in football, but it doesn't have to be like that. I see it in the academies now, where kids are treated like cattle, and then cast off in their formative emotional years. The trauma of rejection implants itself into people at that age and it can affect them for the rest of their lives. It makes me so angry. But John was the better part of football.

You know, football is a vicious, corrupt, and often deeply unpleasant business. It's almost like a war where the casualties are merely collateral damage. Those lucky few that are in favour are flavour of the month and those that are not? Well fuck 'em, seems to be the thinking. It's a very tough, ruthless, corrupt industry and if you have any weaknesses at all, then football is going to have you for breakfast. And that's as a player and as a manager. John Charles' weakness was that he was just too nice. I'm glad he was though, because meeting him and working with him was something I wouldn't want to have missed out on. He was a truly decent human being. I just wish that I could have seen him at the peak of his powers.

He did me once though! He really did me! I was down there in Hereford, I had no bloody money and I needed a car. My one had packed in and I couldn't afford to replace it. John says, "I've got a car, I'll let you have it. I'll let you have it cheap." So he sold me this old car for £50 and, I tell you what, he over-charged me by about £55! This car was so bad it was always going wrong. I was driving back from training once, down this dark country road and all of a sudden I hear this noise. Bang! Bang! Bang!

I'm thinking, what the fuck? So I stopped the car, lifted the bonnet up and the rim alongside the engine, the bit that the bonnet rested on, had fallen into the bowels of the car and was scraping along the road! Yeah, I'll never forget John Charles, but every time I think of him, I think what a lovely man and what a shit car!

I remember when he died. You could tell the measure of the man by the huge amount of people who came out to tell their stories, pay their tributes and grieve for him. For my part, it was simply an honour to have worked for him for a short time.

People are sad when other people die, but that's because they don't understand what death is, it's just a release from this body. I've read so many accounts of near death experiences of people who've died and been brought back to life and what they experienced in between. I've yet to read about one who wanted to come back. Not one, not fucking one.

It's like being put in this reality, is a bit like being a wild animal free to roam wherever you want and then being put in a cage in a zoo. Our consciousness becomes entrapped by density; energetic density, vibration density, which is what this place is, and within this density, it does not have the ability to express its true form, which is the wild animal, able to go where it likes. Free. So, when we leave this body, we are free from the cell. We have so lost touch with the nature of who we are and where we are, that we are actually sad for people when they die. I mean, they're cracking the bottle open up there, you know what I mean?

The more I understand about the nature of life as it is against the nature of life and the way we think it is, the more I see that it's quite a simple process. Whatever we believe to be reality, turn it over 180 degrees and there's what it's like, there's what it is. Black is white, you know?

John Charles died in 2004 at the age of 72. He had battled cancer and heart problems for several years. His passing sparked an outpouring of genuine grief and loss from all of football, especially in Wales and Italy.

"John was without question the greatest footballer produced by Wales," said David Collins, the General Secretary of the Welsh Football Association. "His all-round ability in the air and on the ground made him equally at home as a centre-forward or a centre-half. Indeed, he could play in any position."

David Icke's knee injury eventually forced him to look for a new career. As a broadcaster, he enjoyed a meteoric rise to the top, moving quickly from regional sports coverage to taking the helm of *Grandstand* and *Sportsnight*. It's no exaggeration to describe Icke in television terms as the Gary Lineker of the 1980s. He was a respected sports presenter with the good looks and tousled grey hair that led some, including my mum, to dub him "the housewives' favourite".

It all came to an end after Icke announced that he had experienced a spiritual awakening in 1990. A disastrous interview on BBC1's *Wogan* show a year afterwards was the final nail in his career's coffin. His name became synonymous with lunacy and he was the laughing stock of the nation. For years afterwards, he told me, he couldn't walk into a pub without people pointing and laughing and his children were subjected to all kinds of schoolyard abuse.

He began to write books at a prodigious rate, recounting his experiences and hitting out at the global establishment for everything from lying about wars to starting them deliberately to keep mankind under the cosh.

"The funny thing is," he tells me as we wait for the SeaCat to take me back to the mainland, "I'm now so established as a writer of this kind of stuff, that online conspiracy theorists in America think I'm actually a secret agent producing disinformation for British Intelligence!"

He laughs uproariously at the thought of it all.

"You just can't win, can you?!"

David Icke's website is www.davidicke.com.

6 ⚽ NIGEL SPACKMAN
Thwarted by the Crazy Gang (1988)

The opulent lounge of the Royal Lancaster Hotel is scattered with important-looking men, all dressed in important-looking suits and sorting through important-looking papers. I pick up snippets of conversation about land prices and planning permissions, burgeoning territories and margins. It's all very impressive, but I feel a little out of place, so I just sit quietly in the corner in my torn jeans, scruffy trainers with my unkempt chin full of untidiness and hair like an off-duty Bulgarian waiter. I'm visibly relieved when Nigel Spackman arrives as in another ten minutes they'd have chucked me out the door on a charge of vagrancy.

Spackman doesn't look out of place at all. He's well turned out and confident, like a young executive on his way up the ladder. The distinct scar across his eyebrow, the cause of which he explains in the interview, is the only feature to suggest a different background.

Spackman is very pleasant company and as affable in the flesh as he is on the television where he appears regularly on the new Setanta Sports News channel as one of the more eloquent and thoughtful pundits on the circuit. As our interview begins I find myself quite impressed that he's made the effort to turn up as he's in possession of the kind of throaty, rattling cough that makes the crockery dance across the table every time he succumbs to it.

Born in Hampshire in 1960, he started his career at non-league Andover before going full-time with Bournemouth in 1980. A midfielder of understated quality and composure, he moved to Chelsea three years later and was a key part of John Neal's promotion-winning side. Spackman was originally more of an attacking midfielder, but eventually became an '80s equivalent of a Pirlo or an Alonso-type player, sitting back and distributing the ball gracefully around the pitch. He soon began to attract attention from the top end of the table.

After a spat with Chelsea manager John Hollins, Liverpool made their move and snapped him up for £400,000. Spackman was whisked up north and made his debut in the 1987 League Cup Semi-Final against Southampton. He was immediately accepted by the home supporters who were quick to see his talents and appreciated his unselfishness and style.

In his first full season, Liverpool clicked into top gear. The departure of Ian Rush left pundits wondering if the Merseysiders could hold on to their place at the summit of English football. Liverpool's response was emphatic. Playing their football with unforgettable, mesmerising style, they took the First Division by storm and looked set to win a historic second double. Only Wimbledon, a small, abrasive outfit who had been a non-league team just eleven years previously, could stand in their way.

It's funny how things work out in football. I'd had a great time at Chelsea, but when Liverpool came in with a £400,000 bid for me, I was delighted. Absolutely thrilled. This was in 1987 when they were rightly acknowledged as one of the biggest and finest football clubs on the planet.

I'd been happy at Chelsea when John Neal was there, but when he got ill, Ken Bates was under some pressure to change the manager. Hindsight's a wonderful thing, but looking back the timing wasn't right for a change. He gave the job to our coach, John Hollins, who was a lovely guy, but probably wasn't ready for the responsibility. We'd finished sixth in the top flight in our first season and we had a good team. We had players like Pat Nevin, Kerry Dixon, David Speedie and the spirit was really good, really close. Unfortunately, when John got the job he must have decided that he was too close to the players and he needed a sergeant-major to replace him and give some balance. Ernie Walley came in and his attitude was, "Do it my way or I'll beat you up." Very old school and not what we needed!

It was completely different from the way John had been. It destroyed the team spirit and upset a lot of people. A lot of players had fallouts with the coaching staff in training and I got into trouble more than most because I was quite opinionated. It wasn't long before I was out of the team.

Then, one Monday morning, I got called in to see the boss. He sat me down and said, "We've had an offer from Liverpool for you and we've accepted it." He told me that I was free to go up to Manchester and discuss terms. I wouldn't have minded, but I'd been up in Manchester the night before for a PFA meeting and I'd driven all the way down to the training ground just to get told to go back again! Why didn't he ring me?!

I called my wife and told her that we were going to be moving house and that was it. She dropped me off at Heathrow Airport and I was met at the gate in Liverpool by Bob Paisley and Tom Saunders. It was extraordinary, getting picked up at the airport by the most successful English football manager of all time. They were smashing guys, absolutely fantastic. Everyone knows about Bob Paisley, but Tom Saunders was incredible as well. A very astute guy; he'd been brought in by Bill Shankly and he knew the game inside out. He was one of those guys that stay in the background, no one ever knows too much about them, but he was very, very good.

At this time, if Liverpool wanted anyone, they got them. They were one of the biggest clubs in the world and it was an honour just to be linked with them, never mind signing for them. The way they played football, the way they were renowned, it's a great football club where the supporters really know the game and it didn't matter what they said to me. No one turned down Liverpool. It was the most amazing experience for me to sign for a world-class team, with world-class players.

When you get to a new club, the most important thing is fitting in. I think all the old Liverpool players from the first Shankly days to the last title-winning side of 1990 will tell you that if you couldn't hack it on the training ground, then you weren't going to make it in the team. The banter in the dressing room, the way that we trained, it was like a game situation all the time.

The first training session was an eye-opener. No one could understand why Liverpool could get away with just playing eight-a-side games every morning and still be at the top of English football all the time. That's because they didn't understand the way we trained. No one wanted to lose, not in training, not at anything. The tempo of the sessions was exactly the same as it was for a match and that's what set us apart. When you've got good players, some of the best players in the world, you didn't need to coach them. You just told them what the formation was and let them go out and play.

I loved being at the club and the style of play suited me very much. It's always easier when you've got top players around you. Obviously when players like Peter Beardsley and John Barnes came in, it went up a notch again. The game was pass and move, which I liked and I actually ended up becoming more of a holding midfielder than an attacking midfielder. Steve McMahon liked to get forward, so I let him go and stayed back to tidy up and get a bit of room to play the ball around a bit. It worked great for me and when I came in to cover for the loss of Ronnie Whelan to injury, I managed to hang onto my place and play for most of the season.

What a season it was, as well. We started with a win at Highbury and then went all the way through to March without getting beaten. We played some magnificent football and, all in all, we went 29 games without defeat. The run came to an end, inevitably, at Goodison Park. It didn't matter though, because the title was wrapped up a few games later with a 1–0 win over Tottenham.

Our highest point came just ten days before we lifted the First Division trophy. We'd actually beaten Forest in the FA Cup Semi-Final at Hillsborough just four days beforehand and we'd played very well. Forest were still a very good team at this point and we were delighted to be in the Final. Our league games were being re-arranged left, right and centre, but the view in the dressing room was, "Bring 'em on!" We were playing so well at that time, we just wanted to get out there and get on with it. So, four days after beating them in the cup, we played them again at Anfield.

Even now whenever I see Stuart Pearce he always says, "Don't mention the game. Don't mention the 5–0." They actually started quite well and I remember Bruce Grobbelaar making a fine save from a Nigel Clough shot. After that, though, it was an amazing performance. Everything just clicked into place and we annihilated them. It could have been more than five. It was the first time the BBC has ever brought out a full game on video. Sir Tom Finney was in the stands and he described it as the best club football performance he'd ever seen. When you hear something like that you think, "Blimey, we must be part of something great here."

One achievement of ours that might not be remembered so fondly was our hit single, *Anfield Rap*. We won the title against Spurs on the Saturday and then we headed down to the studio to make the record. We had a lot of beers that day and I think we needed them. It must have made us sound better. It was a weird day. We were all dressed up in shell-suits and sunglasses for the video, with chains hanging around our necks!

It was Craig Johnston's idea. He wrote the song and arranged it, much to the annoyance of the gaffer, because he was taking time off training to do it. Poor old Craig wasn't getting in the team much at the time and if you listen to his section, he makes a plea to Kenny Dalglish for more first-team football!

Everyone got involved. We had Bruce Grobbelaar rapping, John Barnes going on about the crowd going bananas, Steve McMahon and John Aldridge giving it the Scouse thing and the rest of us getting involved where we could. My role was to jump in front of the camera and say, "And I'm from London, mate, so watch your game!" Best lyrics ever.

I can remember when we were doing the singing bit in the studio and we had to wait for the Irish lads to record their line first. Me and Jan Molby sat outside drinking beers, but they couldn't get it right! It took them an hour to say the line, "Don't forget us Paddies." Can they get it right? Of course they can't. By the time me and Jan got on the microphone, we were hammered!

Craig got all the royalties; we just got a few beers. It went to number three in the charts and if we'd have beaten Wimbledon it probably would have taken the top spot. It was great fun to do, but I think Craig had the most fun, because he must have made a small fortune out of it!

Morale was high as we approached the Cup Final. We knew a lot about Wimbledon and the way they played their game. There was no lack of respect on our part. They were a small club and they had a method of playing that worked for them and that deserved respect. If they'd tried to play like us, they wouldn't have managed it, so they did what they were good at which was putting the ball in the mixer and chasing everything. The thing about Wimbledon is that people go on about them being a long-ball outfit and all that, but most of their players went on to do well at big clubs, so they can't have been that bad.

You know what football's like though, nothing's ever simple. One week before the Cup Final we had to play the last of our re-arranged games, at home to Luton Town. Some of the players needed a rest, so Kenny put me at centre-back alongside Gary Gillespie.

Now, Gary will tell you that it was all my fault, what happened next. This high ball came in and Gary called for it. Unfortunately, I was running backwards at the time and I couldn't stop. We clashed heads in mid-air and tumbled to the ground with a thump. I remember lying there on the floor thinking, "Oh God, that's sore." I put my hand up to my forehead and I was bleeding heavily. I didn't think it was that bad and I told the physio to stick a plaster on it and let me carry on. He wasn't having any of it though and both of us were ordered off to go and see the doctor.

We were both helped into the treatment room and left alone, me and Gary both stretched out with ice-packs on our head and him going, "Bloody hell, what did you do that for?" We still have the argument to this day and I always get the blame.

So the doctor comes down and has a look at us and he says that we both need stitches. He looks at the wounds and he says, "Gary, yours is worse, so I'll do you first." He gets cracking straightaway and he doesn't use any anaesthetic because it's a head wound. Gary's sat there going, "Jesus Christ! Ow!" and all the rest of it and I'm watching from the other side of the room going, "Actually, doc, I reckon you could just stick a plaster on this, eh?"

They kept us in hospital overnight for observation and that was when we realised that we might be in trouble. You don't want to be a few days away from a Cup Final with a head full of stitches. All the press were trying to get to us to find out how bad it was and whether we'd miss it and it was touch and go for a while. Gary had had appalling luck with injuries and always seemed to miss the big games, and I was scared because this was my first FA Cup Final and I didn't want to be ruled out at such a late stage. We didn't know for sure until the night before the game. Roy Evans and Ronnie Moran had me out in the hotel corridor, bandaged and strapped up and trying to head footballs back to them.

They were going, "How's that feel? Is that alright?" and I'm nodding and thinking, "Fucking hell, that hurt!"

But every time they threw that ball, I nodded it back and tried not to grimace. I didn't want to miss the match and I knew that if I played, the adrenaline would protect me from the pain. Me and Gary both made the starting line-up, but only if we wore the bandages. Gary got first choice and got a nice subtle white one, I got stuck with a red and white stripy thing.

When Princess Diana shook my hand before the game she said, "What's that on your head?" I told her that the gaffer told me I was playing at Wimbledon, not against Wimbledon and she starting laughing.

Everything was fine before the game in the dressing room. There were a few of the boys in the team who were up for it, and a few who'd been left out who were a bit down. So many of the lads had been there before at Cup Finals that we felt like we were going out and we were going out to win. There was no extra pressure, despite the fact that we were overwhelming favourites. We certainly didn't think that all we had to do was turn up and we'd win. We went through the normal stuff about set-plays, but the overall message was to go out, enjoy ourselves and play our game. But Wimbledon made it very difficult for us.

I keep hearing all this stuff about what Wimbledon did in the tunnel and how they supposedly out-psyched us and it makes me laugh. It's total rubbish. All you do in the tunnel is get your head straight, stare up at the light and ignore everything around you. People were shouting, but that's normal for any game and it all went straight over my head. We were all experienced players and we weren't going to get out-psyched with a bit of shouting. Looking back, I can't even think of anything they said that sticks in the memory, to be honest. We just wanted to get out of the tunnel and start playing football.

Once I'd headed my first ball, I was fine. Same with Gary, we got straight into the game. We should have taken the lead as well. Peter Beardsley scored a perfectly good goal only to have the play called all the way back, so we could have a free-kick outside the box. I still wonder why the referee did that and I think everyone else does too. That would have put us 1–0 up and I think then you'd have had a very different game. You can criticise the referee, but that's the way football goes sometimes. We can't use it as an excuse.

To be honest, Don Howe got the tactics spot on for them. They managed to nullify John Barnes with Dennis Wise, who was a nasty little git sometimes, but a hell of a player! It was him who put a perfect free-kick in to our box and then Lawrie Sanchez flicked it in on goal. My first thought was that Bruce would save it, but looking back at it, it went right in the corner and he never had a chance. I saw the net ripple and I just thought, "Oh. They've scored." We couldn't get upset about it. We just had to pick ourselves up and get back in the game.

In the second half we thought we had, when John Aldridge won a penalty, but it really wasn't our day. Dave Beasant had obviously studied Aldo's penalty taking and he threw himself to his left and made a great save. It was a good height for him and it wasn't Aldo's best spot-kick, but it was still a great save. We had one more chance where we just couldn't poke the ball in the net after doing all the hard work and it got to a point where we were thinking, "God, we're never going to score." But we didn't give up. It wasn't the Liverpool way to start lumping it up front; we carried on trying to pass our way to victory.

In the dressing room afterwards it was horrible. Everyone was disappointed and we were all sat there, heads bowed, in absolute silence. John was distraught. He was a scouser and it hit him hard. He knew that he was the first person to miss a penalty in a Cup Final and no one wants that. He was devastated. Then Ronnie Moran, Roy Evans and Kenny came in.

I think it was Ronnie who said, "Look guys. You've had a fantastic season, you've played some fantastic football, you've won the title. Don't let this overshadow what you've achieved." It helped, it did help, but it didn't change anything and it didn't stop the evening and the dinner afterwards being a real low ebb. We just had to keep reminding ourselves of everything we'd done.

We should have won the double. We were good enough to win the double, but we didn't perform on the day and Wimbledon deserved to win. You can't take anything away from them.

The thing is, football is always changing, always evolving and it's difficult to judge one team against another. There have been some magnificent Liverpool teams in the past 40 years, from the Shankly era all the way through the decades and you just can't compare them directly. The big thing about Liverpool Football Club, the thing you always notice, is the mutual respect between the generations. When we older players meet up for get-togethers and have a few drinks, there's always that respect there. Wherever you look, there's always someone who's won some of the greatest honours in the game, people who've won in Europe. That's why Liverpool fans are so desperate now to get those glory days back.

I think that with the squad of players we had, with the strength in depth we had, we would have been able to win the European Cup in 1988 as well. It's a shame really. If we'd beaten Wimbledon, if we had have won that double, I really think people would have looked at that generation as one of the best of all time.

Liverpool won the FA Cup the following season but, coming just weeks after the tragedy of Hillsborough, it was a hollow victory; 96 people lost their lives in the disaster of April 15, 1989, and it sent shockwaves through the entire game. Football teams across the country ripped down their perimeter fences and the subsequent Taylor Report saw the creation of all-seater stadiums.

Kenny Dalglish left the club in early 1991, citing stress as a reason for his departure. He, along with the first team squad, had been present at many of the funerals across Merseyside, trying to help the region to bear the pain and, quite understandably, he had lost his desire to carry on.

Liverpool had won the title for the final time in the 1989/90 season and when Graeme Souness arrived as permanent successor to Dalglish, he dismantled the squad and attempted to build a new one, with limited success. At the time of writing, Liverpool were in the eighteenth year of their title drought.

Nigel Spackman left the club at the end of 1988, moving to Queens Park Rangers in search of regular first team football. His last start for Liverpool was, ironically enough, against Wimbledon.

"I was very proud to have played for Liverpool and, in hindsight, I should never have left. The problem was that back then there were only two subs and there was a lot of competition for a place in the team. Sometimes in life, you make decisions that cause you to look back and think, 'Why did I do that?' I was a part of something special at Anfield. It was only when I left that I realised how special it was and what a mistake I'd made in leaving it."

Spackman left QPR after just 30 appearances and went north of the border to Rangers where he was able to win even more medals. A final spell back at Stamford Bridge awaited him in the early '90s, before he moved to Sheffield United and later became their manager.

Spackman has had appalling luck in management. He left The Blades, a club he loved, because of boardroom influence. He went to Barnsley and was sacked after only a short period and then he took the wheel at troubled Millwall for just ten games before becoming yet another of their casualties. It could have been worse. He lasted ten games longer than one of his predecessors at The New Den, Steve Claridge.

"I tried to bring the things I'd learnt at Anfield to my teams but unfortunately I haven't always been allowed to manage. I had a board at Bramall Lane who liked to get involved on the footballing side a little too much and started selling players from under my feet. I thought Barnsley was the right club, but that wasn't the case and Millwall speaks for itself. If the right job came along, I'd certainly consider getting back into management, but for now I'm just enjoying my work in the media."

Nigel Spackman is now a respected football analyst working for a number of broadcasters including Setanta Sports News.

7 ● RON ATKINSON
Turning Villa Around (1991–1994)

When Ron Atkinson walks into the lobby of the Bromsgrove Hilton, everything grinds to a halt. The hotel is hosting an Asian business conference and up until this moment the room has been a cacophony of caffeine-fuelled chatter about "revenue streams" and "client bases". As Atkinson saunters through the front door, it all ebbs away into hushed whispers and stares.

"Alright, son?" says the former Manchester United boss to a pointing bystander. He offers his hand and the young businessman eagerly shakes it, but not before nervously glancing to his companion first.

Atkinson has this kind of effect on people. He's a big man in every sense of the word. For decades he has loomed into people's living rooms, not just as a manager, but in his other guise as a ubiquitous pundit as well. Of course, he's been a lot less ubiquitous since he dropped a N-bomb on ITV, but if his small screen exile has broken his spirit, he's certainly not showing it.

When I called him to ask him for an interview, he umm-ed and ah-ed for a while and then told me that he'd call me back. This usually means a no. I had just returned to my contacts book to scramble for a replacement when my phone rang.

"Hello, young man, it's Ron Atkinson here," he barked. "I've got a column to write and you're going to help me."

"Of course," I stammered. "What can I do?"

"I've got to pick out the best three signings of the summer and tell people why they're going to be so successful. Let's see how much you know about football."

I'm ashamed to say that I babbled away for a full 15 minutes, promoting about 37 different acquisitions with nothing more than a vague, "I've heard he's pretty decent."

Thankfully, it must have worked.

Ron Atkinson first came to prominence as a manager in the late 1970s when he led West Bromwich Albion to the top flight. Undistinguished as a player, he was anything but in the dugout. His success at The Hawthorns led to five years in the Old Trafford hot-seat where he won two FA Cups, but couldn't deliver the league title that the fans craved.

After another short spell at Albion, he enjoyed a bizarre period at Atletico Madrid, where he lifted the side from the relegation zone to second place in three months and was promptly sacked by the eccentric President Jesus Gil. He returned to England to manage Sheffield Wednesday and after first experiencing relegation, he rebuilt them and took them back to the First Division.

I told Ron at the beginning of our conversation that the next chapter in his life was his career in a nutshell. "Take over a struggling team," I ventured nervously, "buy shitloads of better players, win some silverware and then get booted out by a twitchy chairman." Thankfully, he agreed with me.

At the end of the 1991/92 season, my Sheffield Wednesday side had won the League Cup at Wembley and secured promotion back to the top flight, but I wasn't going to be the man to take them there. You see, I'd always wanted to be the manager of Aston Villa; they were my team when I was a kid. I'd been approached on two or three occasions in the past, but the timing was never right. I was actually based in the Midlands back then and I used to drive past Villa's training ground on my way to Sheffield. I was always think-ing, "God, if I worked there, I could have had an extra couple of hours in bed!" Yeah, it had always been my ambition to be their manager at some point in my career.

Now, I had a phone call at the end of that season from a respected journalist in the Midlands sounding me out about the job. I said to him, "You know what? I think the time is right."

I'd done three years at Hillsborough and I'd only really intended to do six months originally. I had wanted to go back to Spain and manage there again, but I ended up sticking around.

The timing actually wasn't that great this time, either, but it never is, is it? It was two or three days before we went on an open top bus ride round Sheffield. Now, in an ideal world I'd have liked to have kept it quiet until after the parade. I wanted to speak to my chairman Dave Richards and see if we could settle it in a civilised manner.

I was on my way to the fish and chip shop and I got a phone call from a local radio show. Now, I'd never spoken to them in my life, by the way, but they'd overheard a mobile phone call. Mobiles were analogue then, y'see, not digital, so people could listen in occasion-ally. Anyway, they'd heard my accountant and someone at Villa discussing the developments. So, they put it on me; am I going to be the next manager of Aston Villa? That was on Wednesday and Friday was the open top bus ride through Sheffield. Now, one of the things I've never done, and maybe it's to my detriment, but if someone's got a story and it's true, I've never just gone "No". I've sort of gone, "Well, there has been talk of it".

It was on the seven o'clock news within an hour.

The next day I went into Hillsborough on the premise that I was going to leave the club. I got there and there were loads of fans outside waiting for me, asking me not to leave. I had a terrific relationship with the chairman and Cliff Woodward, another director, and they were quite upset. In the end, they talked and talked and talked and browbeat me.

I'd been in turmoil for two days and they browbeat me until I just cracked and went, "Oh, alright, I'll stay."

It's funny, you know, the little things that can change your mind. On the open top bus, one of the directors, who I think wanted to make some political capital out of it, got on the mike and started slandering Doug Ellis. That rankled with me a bit, that, actually. Seems strange, I know, me getting upset at someone having a pop at Doug! It just seemed unnecessary.

Sheffield Wednesday had offered everything to keep me. Dave Richards had even told me I could have my own Rolls-Royce and driver if I stayed! Just imagine me turning up to watch a third division game in a huge car like that, eh? I was killing myself laughing!

So, I was sat in my garden that weekend, more or less resigned to the fact that I'd be staying in Sheffield, and then someone opened the back gate. It was Doug Ellis and his secretary Steve Stride. Apparently, Doug walked you round his garden when he was going to sack you. Now here he was walking me round mine, which I suppose meant that he wanted to hire me! In actual fact, he was very persuasive. What I didn't know was that Steve Stride, the best secretary I've ever had, by the way, he'd called my wife and asked what it would take to bring me to Villa Park. She'd just said, "Well, make him an offer he can't refuse." I didn't find that out until two years later! She was the best agent I ever had!

I decided to take the job and I went to see Dave Richards to hand in my resignation. That was it. I left it to the clubs to fight it out over compensation. They did alright out of it though, they got a couple of hundred grand for me.

So off I went to Villa. Now, just before all the senior players came in for pre-season, I went down to the training ground and all the apprentices were there. I've always thought that the best way to get to know the kids is to play football with them. There was a few staff in, Jim Walker, Peter Withe, Andy Gray and all that for our team, and Tony Cascarino, who's only come in for a bit of early training to get his fitness back. Now, it's five-a-side and we're all pretty decent, but Tony is having an absolute mare. I kept looking at him and looking at him and at the end I said to Andy, "I tell you what, we've got to get rid of him before anyone sees him play!"

I didn't find this out until years later, but after that game, Tony went in to see the physio. They always confide in the physio. He says, "Jim, I don't think I've done meself too many favours here, have I?" He wasn't wrong! Terrific lad, Cas, but we sold him to Liam Brady at Celtic for £1.25 million not long after that.

I had some good players and some not so good players who turned up for pre-season and it was clear some new blood was required. Paul McGrath was there and I obviously knew him very well from when I had him at Manchester United. The thing was ... now, I've just read his book, y'see, and it's a blinding book, but I've got to say that I didn't know quite how severe his problems were. We knew there were some problems, but reading that, you'd think, "Bloody hell, was he ever sober?" It wasn't like that though. For long periods he just wouldn't have a drink and then all of a sudden

...well, you know the rest. Jim Walker had this uncanny knack of knowing when he was going to fall off the wagon though. He used to say, "Be on your toes, Boss, something's going to happen."

I knew Paul was drunk during a pre-season friendly in Ireland. We'd made him captain for the day because there were thousands of Irish fans in the stadium to see him play. It didn't take long for me to realise that something was seriously wrong. He was distinctly out of sorts, if you know what I mean. After 20 minutes I called Gordon Cowans over and said, "Quick, tell McGrath he's hurt his ankle. Tell him to go down, he's hurt his ankle." And off he came!

I'd spoken about getting rid of him, to be fair. Liam Brady had offered me £750,000 for him that summer. I tell you what, if he'd have gone to £1.5 million, I'd have sold him. That was a very lucky escape for me. Oh, but he was brilliant at Villa. In the first four years of the Premiership, he had one of the best appearance records of anyone. And he was fantastic almost every time. What a performer.

When the fixture list came out, I just laughed. Opening game: Sheffield Wednesday against Aston Villa. God, the one thing you've got to have in football is a sense of humour. My first thought, and I'm not even sure now, is "Someone's been a bit mischievous here." Building up to the game, there'd been all this talk in the papers: Judas this and Judas that. We thought it was all a big joke. I remember Andy Gray saying that he wasn't going to sit next to me on the coach in case someone had a repeater and wanted to have a shot at me! Death threats? Ah, it was all bollocks, wasn't it? And by the way, I had my driver and he was the security man. I knew as soon as the coach pulled up, him and his men would be there. But look, it was nowhere near as hostile as people made out. I had a few in the crowd who had a pop, but I'd actually had a lot wish me well.

The game started and they absolutely battered us. We were 2–0 down in six minutes. Two going on ten, by the way! The fans were absolutely loving it, seeing me get my comeuppance. Somehow we kept them from scoring again for 40 minutes, but we had seven players making debuts and it looked as if they'd never met each other until ten minutes before the kick-off. Well, more like ten minutes after the kick-off actually!

Andy had been doing some TV work in Scotland and he told us that if we put pressure on Chris Woods at crosses, he wouldn't like it at all. He'd been injured recently and according to Andy, he wasn't the same goalkeeper anymore.

We had big Cyrille Regis, who I'd taken on a free from Coventry when they all said he was washed up. He weren't the Cyrille that I'd known previous, but he was still useful. Just before half-time, he went in on Woodsie at a cross and rattled him to win a corner. That was the first time we'd been able to get near him! The corner came in and Woods didn't even go for it. Cyrille banged it in for 2–1 right on the stroke of half-time.

I told the lads at half-time that the game was wide open and if they wanted to win it, they could. We were a different side in that second half. All the inhibitions went out of them. Dalian Atkinson scored a great goal to make it 2–2 and then Steve Staunton ran up the other end on a break and we won 3–2.

Ha! There wasn't much stick being handed about after that, you could have heard a pin drop at the end of the game. Our dressing room wasn't so quiet though! We were staying at a health farm at the time and after all the interviews were done with, we went back and had some very unhealthy drinks. That was our season off and running. We came seventh that year and we felt we were beginning to get a very useful side together.

The next summer, in came Ray Houghton and Dean Saunders from Liverpool and they turned out to be fantastic signings. Saunders and Dalian Atkinson hit it off instantly, they were on fire; absolutely unstoppable. We just kept picking up results in that second season and, though I tried not to think about it too much, suddenly we were in a title race. We were doing really well that year, and all the pressure was on Manchester United. After signing Eric Cantona, it was the year that they had to finally win the title and no one really took our challenge too seriously. I just kept telling the players, "Let's keep pegging away, lads."

You know, if you ask anyone at Villa Park, they'll still say that that 1992/93 side produced some of the best football ever seen there. Everyone was playing with freedom, I used to encourage them to get the ball and go do something with it, express themselves. Remember that goal by Dalian Atkinson where he ran the length of the pitch? Remember Saunders doing his head in, screaming for the pass all the way? That was Dalian; he could only ever score great goals!

But it wasn't to last. Dalian got injured and though Dwight Yorke tried hard, it wasn't the same. We knew it was all over on that Easter Saturday. We were held to a draw by Coventry, not a great game, but as I came off the pitch I was told that Manchester United were being beaten 1–0 at home by Sheffield Wednesday. I got to the top of the stairs and it was still 1–0. I'm looking at my watch thinking, "Hang on, it's ten to five!" and then someone near me went "Oh … they've equalised." I said, "I tell you what, they'll win now. They'll play till they win." And they did. You probably remember seeing Fergie and Kiddo [Brian Kidd] dancing across the pitch afterwards.

My mate, Carlton Palmer, played in that game and he said he went up to the linesman and asked how much injury time there was. The lino's said, "Two minutes." Carlton's said, "Six minutes later, we were still winning 1–0!" That was really the moment I thought, "Oh, hang on a minute. Hang on a minute."

They set off then. Defeat at home would have knocked them back, I'm sure, but after that win, they won almost every game. It had kick-started them. In all fairness, they were a better team than us, but for a long period of the season we played better than them. If you ask anyone connected with the club at that time, they'll tell you that we would have won the title if Dalian hadn't got injured.

We lost the last three games, so the margin of defeat is a bit false in the record books. But when we sat back and reflected that summer, we thought, hang on a bit, we've come runners-up. It would have been nice to win it, but two seasons ago this club was close to going down.

The next season we never quite got the fluency back. I signed Andy Townsend and we became quite solid in the midfield. We were decent, very decent, but our best performances were on the League Cup run that year. We beat Arsenal comfortably at Highbury, we beat Tottenham and then we got Tranmere in the Semi-Finals. Now everybody thought that was the plum draw, but that wasn't the way we saw it up at Prenton Park when we were 3–0 down in the first leg! The funny thing was, we'd absolutely battered them, but they just kept coming up the other end and scoring. Then, in the last kick of the match, Dalian Atkinson popped up and scored to make it 3–1. That goal changed everything; it turned the tie on its head because it meant that we could go through if we beat them 2–0 at Villa Park. When a lower league team beats a top-flight team 3–1, you expect huge celebrations, but Tranmere were dead in the dressing room afterwards. We were the ones who were happy with the result.

The second leg at Villa Park was arguably one of the most dramatic games I've ever seen, let alone been involved in. We did everything right in the first half and we got those two goals inside the first 25 minutes. Then, they came back at us. John Aldridge burst into the box and Bosnich brought him down. Looking back, Bosnich probably should have been dismissed, but the ref let him off. Aldo put the penalty away and it was 2–1.

The game was just slipping away from us when Dalian Atkinson headed in a late, late goal to force extra-time. It was all very tight and then with the last kick of the match, Tranmere's Liam O'Brien, who I'd had as a kid at Man United, hit a free-kick in on goal. It crashed against the post, went behind Bozzy and rolled against the other post. I was just sat there thinking, "Well, that's got to go in". But it didn't. It went to penalties and then sudden death penalties and when Mark Bosnich made his third spot kick save, we were through to the final. What an incredible game.

Mark Bosnich is, and I've said this before, the best goalkeeper I've ever worked with, and I've hardly ever even seen a better one. Andy Townsend and I, when we used to do TV together, someone would always say, "Oh, what a great goal," and me and Andy would look at each other and go, "Bozzy would have got that".

He should never have gone to Man United. That was his biggest mistake. He'd been there before as a kid and he should never have gone back. That might be the only press conference when he's signed a player that Fergie's never been to and that tells its own story. They took advantage of him on a free, I reckon. They wanted Edwin van der Sar and I think it's one of them where there's a very good goalie there on a free and they've taken a chance.

Something wasn't right up there for him. We were astonished by the rumours that they couldn't get him to work in training. We couldn't stop him working! We couldn't get him off the training ground at the end of the day! We used to say, "For Christ's sake, we're closing up, hop it!"

Of course, who do we meet in the final? Only Manchester United! Now, we had a few things to think about here. We knew that we couldn't man-mark Eric Cantona. We'd tried it at Old Trafford earlier that season with Earl Barrett. Earl was a good marker; he kept him quiet for almost the entire game. Just a shame that on the only two occasions Cantona got free he scored twice!

We also knew that we had to match them in midfield. We had Townsend and Richardson who were strong, but I decided to throw young Graham Fenton in as well to pack the midfield. That way their triangle of Cantona, Ince and Keane could be contained by our midfield three. That strength meant that Cantona spent most of the game stuck in traffic.

By moving Dalian Atkinson and Tony Daley out to the flanks we would have unbelievable pace. Steve Bruce and Gary Pallister were great defenders, but they didn't like it when people ran at them. The only thing was that it left poor Dean Saunders isolated up front. I said to him, "Deano, you're just going to run about and run about and run about today and if you get knackered, just wave and we'll put someone else on and he'll run about instead. Don't expect any support from anywhere, you've got to do it on your own, OK?" Bless him, Deano was just like, "Alright, gaffer!"

It worked out perfectly. With goals from Saunders and Atkinson, we were 2–0 up, even though they made most of the early running. With not long left, Sparky [Mark Hughes] got one back for them, but even then I thought we'd be alright. McGrath and Shaun Teale were excellent; no one was getting any change out of them. Then right at the death, Kanchelskis handled the ball on the goal-line and was sent off. Bit unnecessary really, we were just happy with the penalty. Saunders smashed home the spot-kick and that was that.

It was wonderful, such a great feeling that my club, Aston Villa, had beaten as good a United team as they've ever had. I never thought of it as revenge for the title race the season before, or revenge for them sacking me in 1986, I just wanted to win. They went on to win the double, but they couldn't get the treble because of us. Their fans didn't half leave the ground quickly after the game, though. We celebrated in a half-empty stadium!

There were no indications at the end of that season that I wouldn't be there for Christmas. Everyone thinks it was a continual running battle with Doug, but it really wasn't. I always thought that he ran a very well appointed football club. The ground was being developed, everything was done right and I found him quite supportive in the transfer market as well. He could be a bit difficult though, to say the least. At the end, one of the things he levelled against me was that I spent too much time on the training ground, which I find amazing to this fucking day!

You know what? The night we won the League Cup, we were having a great time with the fans and he was sat there looking miserable. I remember someone saying that he'd have been happier getting beat and having everyone hanging around him. But that was the biggest problem Doug ever had with me; I was more popular with the fans than he was.

Doug Ellis's feud with Atkinson became critical the following season. Despite impressing in the UEFA Cup, eliminating Inter Milan on penalties, Aston Villa suffered a poor start in the Premier League.

Atkinson looked to have turned a corner in November when Villa were leading Wimbledon 3–1 away from home.

"Then Andy Townsend got himself sent off," he laughs. "He's a big mate of mine now, but whenever I see him, I slaughter him. 'You got me bloody sacked!'" Wimbledon came back and won 4–3.

Ron Atkinson left Aston Villa on November 10, 1994.

"Earlier that week Doug had been on *Football Focus*," he told me. "'Ron Atkinson is one of the three best managers in the game.' So, three days later when I got the sack, I figured he must at least have Fergie or George Graham lined up!"

Instead, it was Brian Little. Three months later Atkinson was back in football, rescuing Coventry from relegation. He repeated the feat a year later before passing the reins to Gordon Strachan and moving "upstairs". The vague Director of Football role didn't suit him and in 1997 he returned to Hillsborough.

Sheffield Wednesday were struggling and Atkinson made his return on a short-term contract until the end of the season with the clear objective of avoiding relegation. He succeeded but Wednesday, perhaps sensing an opportunity to redress the karmic balance, didn't offer him an attractive new deal and instead handed the job to Danny Wilson.

His final assignment was the impossible task of keeping a free-falling Nottingham Forest side in the Premier League, but it proved too much even for him. Forest slipped into the second flight and never came back.

A comfortable retirement in punditry beckoned, but in 2004, believing the microphone to be switched off, he made the comments about Marcel Desailly that cost him his career, and he paid the price with his portfolio of lucrative columns and TV slots.

Atkinson reappeared in 2006 on the bizarre, but wonderful, Sky One series, *Big Ron Manager*, where he was brought in to help behind the scenes at Peterborough. The ensuing chaos at London Road obviously reminded him of what he'd been missing, as he popped up not long afterwards at Conference North side Kettering, where he began his managerial career.

Atkinson was installed as Director of Football to advise young black manager Morell Maison. When Kettering narrowly missed out on promotion, Maison was fired. Atkinson had repeatedly tried to convince the board not to dismiss him and when they made their decision final, Big Ron, the man still derided as a racist in many quarters, resigned his position in protest.

Ron Atkinson's autobiography, *A Different Ball Game*, is published by André Deutsch.

8 ⚽ BRYAN ROBSON
26 Years of Hurt (1992–1993)

When I arrive at Sheffield United's training ground, Bryan Robson is in the middle of a long meeting with his scouts. This gives me the opportunity to prowl around the complex. Prowling is very high on a list of a journalist's favourite pastimes, it's just behind drinking and complaining and some way in front of working.

The academy is spotless and enormous. The array of glittering youth trophies in shiny cabinets and the scores of trainees wandering around indicates that The Blades are a club very much aware of the importance of planning for the future. Relegated by a single goal at the end of the 2006/07 season, owner Kevin McCabe hired Robson to ensure that that future was spent in the top flight.

The club's canteen sits on a level above a huge indoor training centre with a large window looking down over the pitch. The crash of footballs against the reinforced glass throughout the afternoon suggests that not all of these youngsters will make the grade.

When Robson appears he repeatedly apologises for his lateness, which he really doesn't need to do, and sets about arranging for a tray of tea to be brought over to us. He's polite and hospitable and has a much stronger Geordie accent than I first expected. He is a veteran of these kind of interviews and it's only when I play the tape back a week later that I realise he sidestepped all of my leading questions by just laughing and nodding, and nodding doesn't come across well on a tape. Crafty.

Still clad in his training kit, he tells me about the club and the plans that he has for it. With the right backing, he says, Sheffield United could not only get back into the Premier League, but also start to contend with the middleweight clubs. What he needs, he tells me, is time to put the foundations down.

Bryan Robson was born in 1957 in Durham and began his career at West Bromwich Albion under Ron Atkinson. He was an exceptional midfielder, strong in the tackle and remorseless up front. A lion with a bubble perm, he was one of the finest players in England and, shortly after Atkinson moved to Old Trafford, Robson followed for a then record transfer fee of £1.5 million.

Manchester United hadn't won the League since 1967 and in Atkinson's five years, though he brought them a brace of FA Cups and a second place finish, he just couldn't deliver the title as well. In 1986 his time ran out.

New manager Alex Ferguson, despite early fluctuating performances, was given time to build his empire, the kind of time that Robson wanted at Bramall Lane and, when the 1991/92 season began, it seemed like the club's patience might finally be about to pay off.

We thought we had a real chance of winning the title at the beginning of the 1991/92 season. The club had gradually been improving and growing in confidence. We were starting to believe that we could do it. In 1990 we won the FA Cup and you could see the change in the players immediately. When we won the European Cup Winner's Cup the year later, beating Barcelona in the Final, our morale went through the roof. To win a trophy like that against a team like them was a fantastic achievement. You can't begin to class yourself as a top player until you start to bring trophies in on a regular basis and to do that you've got to play against the best teams in the world and win.

By the time that season started, we had confidence and self-belief in abundance. We also had young, up-and-coming players coming through the team like Paul Ince and Lee Sharpe. We went into that season feeling unbeatable.

Those trophies had given Sir Alex a lot more security, though I don't think he ever felt that his job was in any jeopardy. The press like to give it the whole "If United had lost to Nottingham Forest in the FA Cup he'd have been fired", but there's no truth in that at all. I spoke to Martin Edwards about it a few years ago. We were having a couple of pints together and he told me that there was never a time when he was planning to get rid of the boss. That's just the media being mischievous, but you get used to it after a while. As soon as results go against people who are underachieving, they'll always get the knife in. That's always happened and it always will.

We had a great start to that season, we didn't lose our first game until October and we won six games on the bounce in the run-in to Christmas. We kept getting told that United hadn't won the title in 25 years. It was mentioned in every interview and every press conference and it started to weigh us down.

Then, on New Years Day, 1992, we got walloped 4–1 at home to Queens Park Rangers. It was a complete shock to everyone, not least to Dennis Bailey, the Rangers striker who hit a hat-trick that day. I didn't play in the game, but I was there in the dressing room afterwards when he burst through the door with the match ball asking for everyone to sign it! It wasn't the cleverest thing anyone's ever done, but it was sheer excitement, so you can't blame the lad.

He didn't get a positive reaction from everyone, but I think most of the players actually obliged. He was just a young lad who'd scored a hat-trick at United, so no harm done. I don't think the gaffer signed it though!

It was at this stage in the season that the pitch at Old Trafford began to fall apart as well. Everybody said it was to do with the lack of sunshine and airflow on the grass after a huge new stand was built. Whatever it was that caused it, the pitch quickly ended up more like a sand-dune. Because of the type of quick, ball to feet passing we were playing at the time, it didn't help us at all.

Anyway, we bounced back from QPR, beating our title rivals Leeds United in the League Cup and then started to string a few wins together again. Unfortunately our success in the cups coincided with a new ruling from the FA that stated that clubs couldn't reorganise games beyond the final fixture of the season. That meant that we had a lot of games in hand and we had to fit them in somewhere.

As the season drew to a close our schedule became ridiculous. At one point we had to play four games in seven days. That's one game every other day! We were beaten twice in the league up until the end of March and then four times after that, including three defeats in our last four games. We picked up so many injuries and we just didn't have time to recover.

Mind you, it was in this period that we heard about Lee Sharpe and Ryan Giggs and what they'd been up to! There were rumours going around the club that Sir Alex had been tipped off about a party at Lee Sharpe's house and he stormed round and found Giggsy there as well. I don't think it was the night before the game, but he wasn't happy about it at all. There was another one with those two as well when the pair of them decided to head out to Blackpool Pleasure Beach. That cost them a week's wages!

Sir Alex expects his players to prepare properly for the big games, not to get distracted with anything at all. He used to come down on them really hard. Giggsy towed the line, or should I say, didn't get caught so much! Sharpey just kept getting found out! He was pretty fair with the senior players as long as he thought that they were behaving professionally. It was always the kids that he came down really strongly with. If you look at the players he has now though, it's clear that it worked. Giggs, Scholes, Neville. They're all playing at the highest level in their 30s.

It really annoys me sometimes when people keep going on about a drinking culture at Old Trafford when I played there. I've always said that, at a certain time, I had a metabolism where I could drink a lot in one night. The thing was, everyone thought we were doing it every night and it wasn't like that at all.

You don't play at the top level until your late 30s if you're not looking after yourself. A lot of the fans understand that if you work hard on the pitch, it's not a bad thing if you have a few beers. The media go over the top about it sometimes, but if you do it at the right time, it's fine. I certainly never drank anything 48 hours before a match.

The rewards in the game now are so vast that, as a manager, I tell my players to look after their bodies and give themselves every chance of making it. Get rest, eat properly, drink the right stuff. You can't say, "Don't go nightclubbing", because if you're a young lad and you're single, you're obviously going to go anyway. So you don't knock your players, you just try and make sure that they do it at the right time.

But there was no way that we could have done anything to prepare our bodies for that final run of games, it was ridiculous. Leeds eventually managed to creep ahead of us. We had to go to

Anfield and win if we wanted to stay in with a chance of winning the title, but we lost 2–0. The disappointment of missing out on a title we were favourites to win was far greater than any pain of losing it at Liverpool. I know there's a fierce rivalry between the fans, but for us it was just a massive disappointment that we'd worked so hard all season and ended up with nothing. The fans were great though. They always believed we were going to win it right up to the end of the season and they gave the players great support throughout.

Leeds were a very different team to us. People always criticised their style, with Lee Chapman up front and direct, long-ball football, but they had a lot of good players. People like David Batty, Gary Speed, Gordon Strachan, Gary McAllister, are all class acts.

But, with no disrespect to Leeds or knocking down what they achieved that year, I do believe that they won because the FA wouldn't let us reschedule our games. Those cup runs had cost us heavily and we couldn't cope with the relentless run-in. If the League had allowed us to put a couple of games back it would have been fine. Our situation did have hidden benefits though. It told Sir Alex that we needed a bigger squad if we were to challenge on all levels.

Over that summer, there were rumours of Alan Shearer joining. I used to come into training early in those days after dropping the girls off at school and the gaffer would have Archie Knox and the coaching staff up in their dressing room for a cup of tea and a chat. Sir Alex used to let me come up and join in the discussions. He'd just sit there and open it up to the room, looking for feedback to ideas. The main subject at that time was Alan Shearer.

Alan had a fantastic career at Blackburn and Newcastle and he's always said that he loved it up at St James' Park, but just think what he could have achieved at United. What a legend he would have been. I think if Alan tells the truth he probably regrets his decision.

The new frontman that did come along was, of course, Eric Cantona. We didn't know too much about him when he arrived at Leeds, but we knew he came with a big reputation. We'd heard that after completing a week's trial with Sheffield Wednesday, Trevor Francis asked him to stay and do another week. Eric was apparently so angry at being asked to prove himself again that he stormed out and turned up at Elland Road.

Cantona was the final piece of the jigsaw for our team. He was an outstanding footballer. He had this incredible composure on the ball and because we were so dominant, we'd always put him in great positions where he'd either score or set someone else up for a goal.

For all the reputation, we found Eric to be great. He mixed in with the lads straightaway and we didn't have a problem with him at all. He was the first onto the training pitch and he'd always stay late to practise even more. Set-pieces, volleys all that type of thing. He was a really dedicated player, but in saying that, he also mixed well with the lads. If we were going for a bit of lunch and a few pints, he'd be there. Mind you, it was pints for us and a glass of champagne for him! Seriously!

The 1992/93 season was a three-way battle between us, Ron Atkinson's Aston Villa and Norwich. It was strange seeing Mike Walker's team there, certainly a bit different to battling it out with Liverpool!

Norwich had a cracking season, but eventually slipped off the pace and we battled Villa all the way to the end. I'd played under Ron when he was the manager at Old Trafford and I think he wanted that title as a bit of revenge. For me, I never thought about it that much. We just wanted to win and with the squad of players we had, we felt unbeatable every time we stepped out on the pitch.

I know that Ron wasn't happy about that crucial game at

Sheffield Wednesday when we came back to win it in a long period of injury time, but I was sub at that game. Wednesday were wasting so much time, as teams do when they come to Old Trafford and find themselves one goal up. I came on with 20 minutes to go and we were charging forward, always looking to get back in the game. The fans were fantastic that day. They could see that we were doing everything except score and they kept urging us on. We had a lot of characters in that team, a lot of resilience and that's why we won. Steve Bruce got the goals, both of them headers. I think he scored quite a few that season actually. That was funny enough, but the best moment for me was watching Brian Kidd sliding across the pitch on his knees. He's with me now and I still remind him of that!

I think we knew we were on our way then. I always say that once you get an advantage and the confidence is high, there's very rarely a slip up. Sir Alex knew his players well and he knew that he could trust them. That team had a bit of everything. Eric loved the camaraderie in the side, but when you look back at us, we were the complete package. Him, Sparky and McClair were great goal-scorers, Kanchelskis and Giggs gave us incredible pace on the flanks. Incey, Keaney and myself gave us aggression in the middle and then at the back we were brilliant. You won't get many back fives as good as them. Schmeichel was such a physical presence that he could deal with anything in the air, and that's only if someone managed to get past Pallister and Bruce. I haven't even mentioned Paul Parker and Denis Irwin. Irwin, in particular, was a great player who could read the game so well.

The balance of the squad was perfect and Sir Alex was just starting to bring through that golden generation of Beckham, Scholes, the Nevilles and Nicky Butt. He always believed, even then, that they were going to be good enough. A lot of the senior players at that time took an interest in the youth team and there'd always be a few of us at their Cup matches. We were a good team, but I don't think anyone will ever equal what that young generation have achieved. Giggsy alone has now got 18 major medals and he's still going strong.

Eventually, we won the title without playing a game. Aston Villa had to beat Oldham on the Sunday just to force us to try and win it at home to Blackburn the following night. A win for Oldham would hand the title straight to us.

I had a few of the lads over at my house for the game and Steve Bruce had another load over at his. It seemed strange being able to watch someone else decide it all, but after 90 minutes we didn't mind too much. Oldham won and sealed it and Brucie called us up straight-away and told us all to get over to his house. So we made our way over and ... umm ... yeah, we had quite a few beers! That night went on for a very long time! Unfortunately, we still had to play Blackburn the next day and, I tell you what, it was just as well it was an evening game! I'm not sure many of us would have managed a 3 o'clock kick-off!

It was a strange game, but the fans made it a fantastic atmosphere. Once the adrenaline got going we somehow pulled through. We'd all managed to get a good sleep-in, so we weren't too bad, but when we went a goal down we all thought, "Oh no!" Sir Alex was nice and calm about it before the game because he knew exactly what had happened, but I tell you something, if we'd have got beat 1–0, it wouldn't have been a happy dressing room, trophy or no trophy! Thankfully we came back and won 3–1, so it was all forgotten about.

It must be the only time that Sir Alex was OK about pre-match drinking! I suppose when you've just won the title for the first time in 26 years, you can make an exception!

I'd been at the club 12 years by that point, and I'd been close on a couple of occasions, but not to have won it that year would have been a huge disappointment. When I went to lift the trophy with Steve Bruce, it was amazing. The length of time since the club's last League win had become a shackle around us all and we were finally free of it. All you ever heard at the club was 24 years, 25 years, 26 years, and it became a burden. They do it to Liverpool now and I know exactly what those players are going through.

Manchester United gave Sir Alex time to build an empire and it paid off. With the foundations for success in place, it didn't surprise me at all that the club went on to win again and again and again.

Bryan Robson left Old Trafford in 1994 to become player-manager at Middlesbrough and he played 25 games for them before retiring to concentrate purely on management. In his first season at the helm, he led the club to the Premier League, but they were relegated again after just two seasons, thanks mainly to an FA points deduction.

Undeterred, Robson simply rebuilt and won promotion, again at the first time of asking. A two-year period of mid-table stability came to a shuddering halt when a horrible start to the 2000/01 season saw Boro rooted to the bottom of the table. Robson took the brave step of calling in the former England manager Terry Venables to help and his decision was rewarded by an instant improvement in fortunes. Unfortunately, in the meantime, the newspapers savaged him for relying on assistance and he left the club at the end of the season.

Sir Alex Ferguson continued to lead Manchester United to success winning an astonishing eight more Premier League titles in the next 14 seasons. The generation of young players that followed Ryan Giggs and Lee Sharpe proved to be every bit as talented as their predecessors and many of them featured in the treble-winning side of 1999.

Robson returned to management in 2003 with a short, but

unsuccessful spell at Bradford City, before going back to The Hawthorns in 2004. Under Robson's stewardship, West Bromwich Albion became the first team to escape relegation after spending Christmas at the bottom of the Premier League. The next season, however, they slipped into the second flight. Robson was sacked in September 2006, just a handful of points away from the play-offs with the bulk of the season still to play.

Robson was appointed as the manager of Sheffield United in the summer of 2007 and, when I interviewed him, he had just begun to turn around a disappointing start to the season. Unfortunately, he couldn't maintain the improvement in form and an inconsistent spread of results saw the Blades languishing some way adrift of the play-off places at the start of 2008. With no improvement in sight, the home supporters turned on him in large numbers and there were demonstrations after matches. On February 14, he left the club.

Sir Alex Ferguson put his first title-winning team together over a long period of time and Robson was in no doubt that patience makes a football club. "I think with some clubs, people allow you time to develop. I had it at Middlesbrough when I went there and Sam Allardyce and Alan Curbishley had it at Bolton and Charlton and look what they achieved. For me, as a manager, you need at least a three-year period to actually impose what you want within a club. I still don't think that the right way to go is to keep changing the boss. You just don't get any cohesion like that."

Unfortunately, Robson wasn't granted the time and patience that his former mentor received at Old Trafford and his hopes of finally stepping out from under Sir Alex's shadow have taken a savage battering. He has now accepted a role as an ambassador for Manchester United while he contemplates his future in the game.

Bryan Robson's autobiography, *Robbo*, is published by Hodder & Stoughton.

9 ⚽ RAMON VEGA
Vilified at Spurs, Idolised at Celtic (1997–2001)

Ramon Vega's handshake is legendary. I'd been warned about it by several people before my first meeting with him but it still caught me by surprise. It's strange that a man who spent his career playing top-flight football across Europe is now renowned for the way he greets people, but when your casual introduction dislocates the shoulders of your new found friends you have to expect to get a reputation. It's extraordinary, it really is. His hand starts up somewhere above his neckline and howls in on yours like a dive-bombing Stuka. By the time you realise what's happening it's too late to brace for impact and you find yourself lifted off your feet. Vega is a big man. Not for nothing was he compared to Mr Universe when he first arrived in English football. He also speaks at three times the speed of most normal people, which was fortunate as his relentless diary left us with only a third of the time I'd decided I needed for the interview. He honestly never stops. If he's not talking, he's twitching or leaning or looking or shuffling. He is the kind of person you suspect would get very bored if he wasn't trying to do at least three things at once.

Vega is an entertaining man to be with. He is delighted when I tell him that Celtic-supporting friends of mine have described him as a cult legend and his eyes all but mist over when he speaks about his time in Scotland. Mention Tottenham, however, and the shutters come down. He is defensive at first and makes it clear that he doesn't blame the supporters for getting on his back, but you can tell that beneath the hulking exterior, it stings just to have to talk about it.

Born in Switzerland in 1971, Vega made a name for himself as a powerful centre-back for perennial Swiss champions, Grasshopper Zurich. His exploits caught the attention of the Sardinian side Cagliari, where he spent a year playing in Serie A.

He arrived at White Hart Lane in January 1997 in a £3.75 million deal and never really managed to win the Tottenham fans over. Despite being part of the 1999 League Cup-winning side, he was mercilessly pilloried from the terraces.

When Martin O'Neill took over at Celtic, he was left with the shattered remnants of the ill-fated John Barnes and Kenny Dalglish managerial dream team. Changes needed to be made quickly and, halfway through his debut season, he decided to call in defensive reinforcements. So damaged was Vega's reputation that even O'Neill's most loyal supporters shuddered with trepidation when he arrived, but this was another masterstroke by the former Leicester manager.

With the manager and the fans behind him for once, Vega went from zero to hero.

When you are a professional footballer and you are being barracked and shouted at from the stands as you try to do your job, make no mistake; it hurts. I would be lying if I said it didn't. I'm a human being and I could hear what they were saying about me. Those last years at Tottenham Hotspur were difficult for me, for sure.

But listen, in the first place I was very happy to join Spurs. I had come over from Serie A and I was excited at the prospect of playing in England. I wanted to learn more about the club, about its history and about its fans. It was clear that Spurs was a very big team, you know, but every club has its own problems and its own politics. As a young player, as a foreigner coming to England, I was not aware of this. When I joined the club, nothing was simple. The club was going nowhere and everything was up in the air all the time. It was too unstable a situation in those days. The fans were furious at the board all the time, shouting and protesting and everyone always felt under pressure.

Since I started working in the financial world six years ago, I've found that every business needs leadership and it's the same with football. The board has to lead the team; they have to set an example for the whole club to follow. They need to lead everyone else in the right direction and not give out mixed signals that can lead to insecurity. If you are a manager, a chairman, a CEO, whatever, the principle is still the same. You must give assurances to your staff, to the people below you and tell them that everything is going to be alright. That leadership simply wasn't there at Tottenham.

The dressing room was a dark place to be. There were concerned faces everywhere you looked. Managers would come and go without being allowed to settle and that unnerves everybody. I played for three managers in my four years at the club, and that's not including the times when David Pleat, the Director of Football, would take over.

Footballers don't like change. You have to remember that the career of a player is entirely dependent upon his manager. One man can walk into the dressing room and say he does not like your face and that is it – get out! When the players are that insecure, you can get a domino effect on morale. When everyone is worried about their career, you are no longer a team. You are a group of individuals playing for yourselves.

Of course, this did not reflect well in our performances and the supporters became angry. It is tough for them. They have to sit up there while we are allowed to be on the pitch. They'd love to be players, but they are not. They can't play, but they can blame.

I saw both sides of the Tottenham fans while I was there. I saw them when they were low and upset, but I saw them happy when I was a part of the League Cup winning team at Wembley.

I played that whole game at Wembley with a broken foot, you know? Nobody knew at the time that I had a stress fracture. After that game I did not play again for nine months, it almost finished my career.

The doctor said, "If you play one more game, you will be finished."

I said, "This is vital for Spurs, I want to play, I want to win." If you see the video clips you can see that I was limping, I could barely walk. I was on painkillers for the whole thing. There was no way I was going to say anything though. Why not? Listen, if I had said before the game that my foot was broken, people would have thought it was an excuse. In my entire time at Spurs I just kept my mouth shut and did my best. That medal is so precious to me because of what I went through to get it.

There's so much potential at White Hart Lane. In terms of history, in terms of what you could do with the club. If I had the money I would love to buy them. I'd give the club a different atmosphere. I genuinely believe that if the board got it together, backed their manager and put on an image, then the supporters would follow. As I say, I ever get the money ...

Anyway, George Graham was very, very good for Tottenham; I was sorry to see him lose his job. I played my best football for Spurs under him and, of course, won the League Cup. The defence was so good with me and Sol Campbell. We were disciplined, we were confident, and when Graham worked with us, he made us feel like a team, but the fans did not like him, and so he goes.

They had their favourite players to cheer and their favourite players to boo. They were difficult fans. Sometimes, even if we were 2–0 up, they would still boo us. After four years at White Hart Lane, I began to realise what the Spurs fans are. They are frustrated. They have so many ambitions and the standard they demand is very high, but they don't get what they expect, so they boo.

It doesn't help the players, but they don't realise that. But in fairness to them, they pay a hell of a lot of money for their tickets and they expect to get something back on the pitch. I would expect something. Sometimes, as well, they have had a bad week at work and they need to let it out somewhere. I understand that. But, that's football. That's the beautiful game.

So, yeah, I was abused. But you know what? I look at the people who booed me and I say, listen. I was lucky. I never lose sight of that. I was in a very privileged position being a footballer. The people in the stands, they would want to do what I was doing. In their wildest dreams, they would want to be where I was. It is sport; it is emotions. Sometimes what they shout does not even mean anything, but then that does not mean it did not hurt me.

Yes, I have mixed emotions and memories of Tottenham. I can understand from the Spurs fans' point of view how upset they were. The club was going nowhere, you know? It was hard for us as players as well. It is frustrating not to get what you want. If you are a sportsman, by your very nature you are competitive; you want to win. If you fail, it hurts.

It was hurting at Tottenham and, in December 2000, I decided to leave. Six months earlier I was told that Martin O'Neill was interested in taking me up to Celtic. I was called into Pleat's office and he said, "Would you like to go there?" I had a contract still at Tottenham though. I wanted to show the Spurs fans that I was a good player. Pleat said that it was down to me. He said, "You can stay here, but if you want to go, you are more than welcome."

Celtic was a flattering offer, but I told him, "No, the time is not right, I want to have my opportunity here." Six months later, it still wasn't working out. So this time when Martin O'Neill called, I said yes. Looking back, it was the best decision I ever made. O'Neill was an amazing manager. When we first met he told me about himself and what he was trying to do at Celtic. He said that he wanted me to be a part of his team and there is nothing better, as a footballer, than to hear someone say that.

He wanted Celtic to be a great club again and he made me believe that he could do it. He is a very knowledgeable man. He was confident and assured and he made a point of telling the players that they were good enough. That's all a player ever wants, you know? You just want a manager who says, "Ramon, I want you. You are part of the team."

I had no idea how big a football club Celtic were when I signed for them. No idea at all! I knew a little about their history and I knew they were one of the biggest clubs in Scotland, but I wasn't expecting to find a team that played on another level. When they went to training camps in America, 20,000 people would turn up to watch them practise!

My first match against Aberdeen was unbelievable. There were 60,000 people in the stadium and the noise was so loud that I had goosebumps all over me. It was like football from another planet and it made my hair stand on end. We went into the pre-match huddle and it felt awesome. I was hooked instantly. No disrespect to the

Tottenham fans, but this was completely different to life at White Hart Lane. When the game started, the fans roared and we tore into Aberdeen. Henrik Larsson scored after a few minutes and then, not long afterwards, I scored. The crowd exploded!

Spurs fans never gave me the best of times, but at Celtic I was part of the family, I was one of them. I was accepted. Here, the fans gave you the strength to go to levels that you did not think you could reach. You gave everything, even when you were in pain, even when you did not think you could go on, you lifted yourself again. 60,000 people all on top of you, cheering for you, carrying you; what a feeling!

I scored again that day and we ended up winning 6–0. It was instant justification for everything that had happened. Martin O'Neill was justified for signing me, I was justified in moving to Scotland and I think maybe it got the Spurs fans' attention as well. But the most important thing was that it made a good impression with the Celtic fans and they welcomed me with open arms. All that in one game; God, it felt fantastic.

Glasgow was an amazing place to live. People would stop me on the street or come over and talk to me in restaurants. Everyone was like, "Nae bother, big man!" That was the only bit I could understand at first, I had so much trouble with the accent!

The Old Firm derby was one of the most incredible experiences of my career. Even when I had played at Anfield and at St James' Park, I had not heard football fans so loud. My first derby game was incomparable to anything else I had ever seen. You can sense the tension in the stands. At Ibrox, you can feel the hatred coming out of the stadium at you. So loud it was magnificent, so beautiful. And when you win ... the green and white is everywhere.

And listen, Martin O'Neill is a great manager and he understands footballers, but if he was not happy, he would let you know.

I experienced that a couple of times! It kind of takes you by surprise, when he shouts, because you think, "Where is that coming from?" It wakes you right up! He's a kind of introverted guy normally, but when he comes out at you, he really comes out, you know? It wasn't shouting so much, as distinct and direct criticism. It was all very well aimed. It doesn't help when a manager just bellows at you, because you don't know what he wants. You just end up thinking, "Well, what did all that mean?" He was constructive and when he criticised you, you felt like you'd let him down personally.

Martin's biggest strength was to give you full responsibility. He did not treat you like you were a little kid; he treated you like a man. Now, the team had some young guys in it and he was giving them the feeling that when they were on the pitch, they must be men. They must not let the team down. They must take responsibility. No one wanted to let him down, that was the feeling he created in the dressing room.

The other players in the team helped as well. There were some great players in that squad. We had Henrik Larsson, Chris Sutton, Didier Agathe. What a team! The atmosphere in the squad was brilliant. We had lunch together; we played golf together. I got there and I thought, "This is what I've been missing, this is what I wanted". I was home. At Spurs we didn't have this so much. We were always being criticised by someone, so everyone was unhappy and moody. There was no team spirit there at all.

Celtic was a dream season. Payback for everything I had been through. For four years I had gone backwards. Before Tottenham, I had had success everywhere, but I went to that one club and it all stopped. Imagine how it felt to be happy again. By the end of May we had won the League, the League Cup and the Scottish Cup. We did the lap of honour and it was wonderful.

I could have stayed at the club; I had an option. Martin O'Neill offered me a one-year contract extension. Unfortunately, I was not the youngest anymore. At 29, you have just one more chance for a good contract. I needed long-term security and a one-year deal just didn't give me that. I wanted to stay forever, you know? I loved it at Celtic. If they'd given me five years, I'd have stayed there for five years. But Martin was honest. He said he was offering a year and if I found anything better elsewhere with long-term security I was welcome to take it. I'll be honest, I felt a little let down not to be offered more, but you have to make the best of it. Watford came in with an offer, a really big offer. So big, actually, that it almost sent them bankrupt. It was a four-year deal with excellent wages so I said, well, OK; I'll go for it. I had to take the decision for my long-term security.

It broke my heart to leave that club. I was so grateful to the Celtic fans for taking me in and making me believe in myself again. They gave me such a welcome and I wanted to stay longer, but that was not possible. But one thing is sure, it was an honour to play for them.

That first month at Watford, I was so very disappointed. I'd come from such a height, playing for a team like Celtic, that it was hard to settle. It was the first time in my life I'd played outside the top flight. Halfway through the season, I knew that I regretted my decision. I didn't want the money; I didn't want the financial security. I just wanted to be back in Scotland.

Spurs were a part of my life, they gave me a chance, an experience at a big club and I owe them for that. But I tell you what; I'd walk to Glasgow today for a chance to play for Celtic one more time.

Like Espen Baardsen, Ramon Vega reached a settlement with cash-strapped Watford and left Vicarage Road prematurely. He had one last club, Creteil in France, and then retired in 2003.

Intriguingly, like Baardsen again, Vega moved into the financial world, working for an asset management firm in London. "Must have been something about working for Alan Sugar," he laughed when I mentioned it.

Duet Asset Management has over £1.5 billion under management and works mainly with hedge funds. "I've been working in finance for five years now and I love it," he beamed. "It was a difficult transition at first and there were a lot of people who didn't think that a footballer would be able to handle it, but I love it now."

Martin O'Neill racked up an astonishing amount of trophies during his five years at Celtic and only called time on his own reign in 2005 to care for his seriously ill wife. In 2006 he returned to English football as Doug Ellis' final appointment at Aston Villa.

Vega is uncertain as to what counts as the proudest moment of his career; the English League Cup win or the Scottish title. "I just don't know," he laughs. "It's two different countries, two different victories. You know what? I think they both are equal, I am proud of them both!"

What is certain is that, one way or another, supporters of either club are unlikely to ever forget him in a hurry.

Ramon Vega now works for Duet Asset Management. You can find out more about them at www.duetgroup.net.

10 ⚽ CARLTON PALMER
Did He Not Like That (1993)

My taxi driver is tremendously excited that I'm going to see Carlton Palmer. "Ah, Carlton Palmer!" he exclaims. "He has been in my taxi many times, he's a very big man around town."

Palmer, of course, is a very big man whichever way you look at him. Six foot three with legs as long as the A1, he towers above me when we meet at a pub near his home in Sheffield. As we wait to be served, he chats with the regulars about the appalling England result in Moscow the night before. There's no air of superiority, no arrogance and nothing to suggest that he is a man who represented his country on 18 occasions in the early '90s.

As we settle into our seats, he tells me that he's very pleased to hear that I've already interviewed Ron Atkinson, a man to whom he is so close that his children "have been sick on his lap".

"You must have got a good story from him," he laughs.

Palmer has never played politics and is fiercely loyal to his friends, as he demonstrated when he spoke out in defence of Atkinson in 2004. Comfortably retired from the game, he runs a number of establishments in Sheffield and appears regularly on the BBC to lend his opinions.

He is intelligent and speaks well about the game, not always eloquently but with passion and insight. I've seen him on Starhub, an international TV station that feeds Premier League football to places like Singapore and Dubai, and he's been so forthright and opinionated that, agree with him or not, you can only applaud him for refusing to mouth platitudes.

Palmer began his career at West Bromwich Albion in 1984 where he played over 100 games before being signed by Atkinson for Sheffield Wednesday in 1989. He won the League Cup with The Owls and promotion for the inaugural season of the Premier League. As a player he was most commonly described as "awkward", but a clutch of Supporter's Player Of The Year trophies from several of his former employers tells its own story. Almost every manager who signed him re-signed him at a later date.

In 1992 Graham Taylor called him into the England squad and gave him a chance to play in a World Cup.

As Steve McClaren's England side struggled through their qualifying games in 2007, a lot of people were quick to draw parallels with the Graham Taylor era. I was part of that team and we didn't qualify for the 1994 World Cup. When Russia beat England in Moscow to ruin England's qualifying campaign, there were all these stories comparing the two teams. The thing is, our generation were a lot closer to qualification than people remember. If it hadn't have been for some really bad luck, it could have all been very different.

I'll always be indebted to Graham Taylor for giving me my first chance for England. I remember when he first called me up to the senior squad for a friendly against Russia in Moscow. My club manager at the time, Trevor Francis, desperately didn't want me to play. We had Sheffield United in the FA Cup Semi-Finals coming up and he didn't want me to get injured. Obviously, I understood his concerns, but this was England we were talking about!

Graham Taylor heard that I might have to pull out and he phoned me up personally. "Carlton," he said, "this is your chance. This is your opportunity. I really need you to come out and play for me." I wasn't sure what to do until he said, "If you come out to Moscow, I guarantee you that you'll play."

I was torn because I obviously didn't want to miss the derby game. It was a huge match for the club, but like any footballer I was desperate to play for England. I thought long and hard about it and finally I went to Francis and said, "Look, I've got to play in this game."

He wasn't happy. He wasn't happy at all. He said that if I got injured and missed the Semi-Final there'd be hell to pay. So I took a deep breath and went out to Moscow with the squad. Graham was true to his word and I played and gave a good account of myself. Unfortunately, I split my toe doing it.

Francis was livid. Oh Christ, he went absolutely ballistic. I was ruled out of the Sheffield derby but I managed to get them to load me up with painkilling injections so that I could play. The physio said that the pain relief would only last 90 minutes, so when that game went into injury time, there must be footage of me somewhere belting down the tunnel of Wembley for a top-up jab! At the end of the game, we won and made it to the Cup Final. Everyone was celebrating but I was in the corner crying. My foot was a right old mess and I had to have all the stitches taken out and put back in again.

Anyway, it was worth it because I was named in the England squad for the start of the qualifying campaign. Right from the opening exchanges we knew that it wasn't going to be a straightforward group. Norway managed to beat Holland in their first game and that made it a three-way race for just two qualifying places. We could only draw with Norway at Wembley after a wonder-goal from Kjetil Rekdal. Now, you can't do fuck all when a guy scores a goal like he does. That was a good point we got there. We didn't deserve to lose, so it wasn't a bad result to open the campaign.

To be fair, the only easy pickings in our group was San Marino, the rest were all very decent teams. At this point we were aware that the press were on the manager's back, but we were all young players trying to make our way in international football and we didn't get too concerned by it. Graham was brilliant to all of us and seemed to be coping with it fine.

We played well in the next few games, picking up the points home and away against Turkey and at home to San Marino, but our first vital game was Holland at Wembley. We really should have beaten Holland, you know. That first 45 minutes was the best we ever played. At the time, John Barnes was getting all kinds of stick, but it didn't bother him. He wasn't the kind of person who let anything bother him. He'd been getting booed by the fans, hammered in the newspapers, but he went out into Wembley, held himself high and stuck a magnificent free-kick into the corner of the net after just two minutes. Twenty minutes later and David Platt's whacked in another one. All of a sudden we're in control against one of the best teams in the world. We was comfortable and we thought, you know, let's just keep this going. But as well as we played in the first half, Holland were so good that they were always going to be able to put us under pressure.

Dennis Bergkamp scored a fantastic goal to make it 2–1 and suddenly we're doing our best to hang on. The clock was ticking down into the final five minutes when Des Walker tugged Marc Overmars back just outside the box. The referee blew for a penalty.

Des was devastated. He knew it was outside the box, we all did. It was never, ever a penalty. We just had to stand there and watch Peter van Vossen put it away.

We played so well that night. At one point, two goals to the good, someone hit the post. I can't remember if it was Wrighty or Les Ferdinand, but we hit the post. Imagine that, we could have been three goals up at half time.

In the dressing room afterwards it felt like a defeat, it was horrible. Graham stood there and tried to put a brave face on it.

"There's not a lot I can say," he told us. "It wasn't a penalty and we didn't deserve to get beat."

But we all knew what that penalty meant. Assuming all the other games went as planned, we had to do better than our rivals. That meant that we had to go to Norway and win and that somehow we had to go to Holland and win as well.

A month later we went to Poland looking for a morale-boosting victory to get us back on track, but we needed a late goal from Ian Wright just to grab us a point. We felt OK though, we knew that we could beat Norway and be back in the ascendancy.

There wasn't much of a gap between the games and we were all surprised when Graham announced a pretty major tactical change. Norway played with lots of long balls all aimed at big Jostein Flo. Taylor decided that the best way to deal with this was to switch to three centre-backs with Pallister on the left, Adams on the right and Des in the centre.

We didn't have much time to work on it though, it was a last minute thing. I had a bad feeling about it and I think we all did. I know that there was genuine concern in the dressing room before the game, but the only person who could tell the manager that things weren't right was the captain. However, the captain was

David Platt and he certainly wasn't going to say anything, so we went out there.

They battered us; they absolutely battered us. There was so much space on the pitch that they scored one before the break and one straight after it. It wasn't all about the formation; most of us were knackered as well. I'd played 70-odd games that season already and I remember walking down the tunnel thinking, "I ain't got much left in the tank".

But I've got to be honest; managers change systems and good players should be able to react to it. I remember once at Leeds, we were off to Arsenal and Howard Wilkinson wanted to switch to 4–5–1. I turned round to him and I said, "Gaffer, you cannot go to Arsenal and play 4–5–1. They've got so many good players you're going to get a hiding. We're going to be inviting pressure and we'll get savaged."

He said, "Carlton, I'm the gaffer. If you do what I say, if you do what I tell you, I guarantee that we'll win this game."

Everyone did what he told them; Phil Masinga scored and we won 1–0. That put me in my place. But it didn't happen in Norway. We just didn't adapt quick enough.

After the game the atmosphere was dead. Everyone was tired and everyone was down. It's alright people going on and on about representing your country and it all being a big honour and everything, but until you've been in that position you just don't know what it's like to be under that pressure. It gets to you, it really does. You sit there and you know you have to fly back, get in, read the newspapers and it will be, "So and so is shit, so and so is shit and you're shit."

Everyone has a bad game at some point and when the criticism comes in it hurts. It really hurts. The press are bad. They build people up and build them up, they get the expectations so high and then when it all goes wrong we all jump in and kill 'em afterwards, it's crazy. There was some pretty nasty stuff about Taylor in the papers. It got really personal and savage. Whatever Graham had done, he didn't deserve to be made a laughing stock of the entire country.

We all had to go off that summer for a tour around America and it was there that I noticed the pressure had really started to take its toll on the boss. The night before our flight out to the States, the boys got together and organised a big piss-up. Nigel Winterburn sorted it all out down at his mate's nightclub in Epping, but Nigel got stitched up. He'd been told that there wasn't going to be any cameras there and that it would be safe for us to let off some steam, but it didn't turn out like that and the tabloids were filled with pictures of us all out on the piss. They absolutely caned us.

Now, as boys, we were always going to be going out for a few drinks and I don't think Graham would have minded that much, it was the fact that it went all over the papers that got him so upset. He went absolutely ballistic at us all when it broke, screaming and shouting and telling us that we'd let him down.

We didn't know at the time that he was being filmed for a documentary. No one knew about it at all because he didn't say a word to anyone. He was miked up for most of the campaign and so many things must have ended up in the public domain that shouldn't have been there. I've never watched it yet and I don't want to. If the squad had known about it there would have been trouble. They'd have all said no. I certainly wouldn't have agreed to it. Some of what appeared was banter, banter when we were all under pressure and you don't want people to see that.

The next season we've gone back to Wembley and taken Poland apart 3–0. Pearce has scored a fantastic free kick, but it's all irrelevant really, because then it was shit or bust in Rotterdam. Naturally, the press weren't being very helpful and no one gave us much of a chance of making it. It was disappointing because we felt that we should have had the whole thing sewn up long before we had to go to Holland. We just shouldn't have had to go to Rotterdam needing to win.

In spite of phenomenal pressure, Graham was brilliant in the build-up to the game. The preparation was good, he picked a similar side to the one that beat Poland and we were set. The only difference was that he switched me onto the right wing and brought Paul Ince inside. That had been a long running problem for the two of us. We both wanted to stay in on the centre but there was only room for one. Incey had done the job before and now it was my turn. I wasn't keen, but you'd rather play for your country than not, wouldn't you? I did the best I could.

We were all over them in that first half. Tony Dorigo had hit the post, we were making lots of chances and we came in at the break thinking that it was only a matter of time until we made the break-through. Graham took me off at half-time and I don't really blame him. I was being cancelled out and I wasn't comfortable out there. He brought on Andy Sinton to give us some width, which seemed like a good move.

Yeah, it was all set up for us to go out there and pick up the points. And then it all went horribly wrong. A fantastic lofted pass released David Platt into space. He charged into the area and was hauled back, clearly and cynically hauled back by Ronald Koeman just as he enters the box.

The ruling bodies had just clarified the punishment for a professional foul by the last defender. It was a red card. If you tugged someone down and prevented them from scoring, then it was a red card. Someone forgot to tell the referee. We couldn't believe it when we saw him standing there holding a yellow card in the air.

Ron Atkinson plays it safe and gets Doug where he can see him. Atkinson was never entirely comfortable having Doug Ellis as a chairman and his fears were justified. Just one month after this picture was taken, he was sacked.

Bryan Robson is crowned by a long-distance truck driver from Louisiana. Oh, alright then, by team-mate Steve Bruce. This photo was taken after Manchester United clinched their first title in 26 years, all the way back in 1993.

Ramon Vega celebrates not playing for Tottenham. The big Swiss centre-back had a miserable time at White Hart Lane, but played an important part in the superb Celtic treble of 2001 when he moved up north. And he got to play with Henrik Larsson.

Carlton Palmer's legs are enormous. Just imagine one of those stretching out at you when you're running through the middle. This is Palmer during Graham Taylor's ill-fated tilt at the 1994 World Cup.

Stan Bowles, away from the stresses and strains of everyday life. Bowles was the shining light at the centre of QPR's unlikely title challenge in 1975/76. They only just missed out, finishing as runners-up.

Skimpy shorts and bleached blonde, bouffant hair. This, ladies and gentlemen, was the zenith of 1980s man. Frank McAvennie was deadly on the pitch for West Ham, but even more successful in Stringfellows. Although, looking at this picture, you probably didn't need me to tell you that.

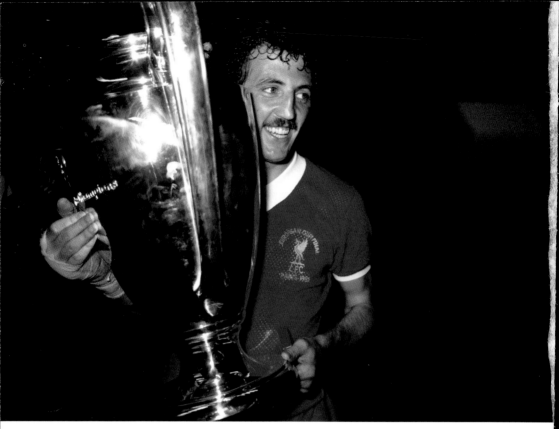

Alan Kennedy celebrates with the trophy that was used to conceal Jermaine Pennant during the Anfield Hide & Seek tournament of 2007. "When in Rome, just beat the Romans," was never a saying until 1984 when Liverpool did it in the European Cup Final.

Tony Woodcock (back row, second from right) and Viv Anderson (back row, second from left) take their place in a squad arranged in order of hair volume. This is Nottingham Forest in 1978, approaching the peak of their Europe-conquering powers. When Brian Clough arrived, they were languishing in the second flight.

Then it got even worse, he didn't even give us the penalty. It was a disgrace, an absolute disgrace. We all knew it at the time and we still know it now.

I was out on the touchline when it happened and I was there with the other subs, screaming and shouting at the linesman. I didn't see this footage of Graham shouting at the fourth official but I've been told about it. I don't blame him, to be honest. First of all he doesn't send the man off, then he doesn't give us a penalty. Just one of the two would have done us.

We drove the free kick into the wall and lost possession. Sixty seconds later and Holland get a free kick on the edge of our box. Guess who steps up to score? Yeah, Ronald Koeman. That's the fine line between success and failure, isn't it?

They stuck another one in David Seaman's near post, just for good measure and that was it. It was a nightmare in the dressing room afterwards. We knew that it was all out of our hands. We had to beat San Marino by seven, which was do-able, but Poland had to beat Holland, which probably wasn't.

Two terrible refereeing decisions, one at Wembley, one out there in Rotterdam and that was it; we were out.

I was left out for the final game, but I was on the bench when it came through that Holland had won. Everyone just knew it was over. It was depressing, you know? Graham said his goodbyes, thanked everyone for their efforts and that was it.

You know what though? I honestly believe it was a relief for him in the end. Relief that he was finally out of it. When you're a proud man and you're publicly ridiculed like he was, it's a relief to get out before it breaks you. It put him out of his misery.

What happened to him was a disgrace. It really affected him. For ages he wouldn't go out, he just wouldn't leave the house. I used to phone him up and say, "Come on, boss, it's over now. Come out, you've got nothing to be ashamed of." I felt so sorry for him; he didn't deserve it. Football's important, let's not beat around the bush, it matters. My wife Lucy, she sometimes says, "What are you getting worked up about? It's only a game!" It's not a game; it's fucking life. But it's life to us, because it's our job. When we lose a match, Saturday night's the worst thing in the world, until we calm down and have a few pints, wake up on Monday morning and do it all again. It's our livelihoods.

But Graham Taylor didn't kill nobody, he didn't do anything wrong and he didn't deserve to get stuck on the front pages and humiliated.

When you look back at it all now, it's clear that he was really a victim of circumstances. After Euro '92 there were a lot of players coming to the end of their international careers, Gary Lineker being the most notable. He had to build a new squad of players, and he lost Alan Shearer right at the start of the campaign to a long-term injury. Imagine what we could have done with Alan Shearer at his peak in that side. Very little went in his favour.

As I say, Graham was a very proud man and it took him a long time to recover from what happened to him. But, I don't think the people hated him as much as the press made out. Someone told me that when he finally went out in public again, he took his wife out to see a show. Apparently, someone noticed him in the crowd and all of a sudden the lights came on. Everyone turned around to look and when they saw it was him, they gave him a standing ovation. After all that he'd been through, it was nothing less than he deserved.

Graham Taylor returned to management in 1994 with Wolverhampton Wanderers, leading them to fourth place in the second flight and an unsuccessful play-off campaign. A poor start the following season meant that he lost the support of the fans and he resigned in November 1995.

When Elton John returned to Watford, he brought Taylor with him as General Manager but it wasn't long before the man who had led Watford up the divisions in the early '80s took the wheel again. In just two seasons he led Watford from the third flight to the Premier League, arguably a greater achievement the second time round. They only stayed there for one season, but not even the most ardent Watford supporter could ever have predicted that he could have brought the limelight back so quickly. Taylor retired from football management a year later, popping up just for one season to provide a steady hand on the Aston Villa tiller. He is now a respected pundit.

The defeat in Rotterdam was Carlton Palmer's last game for England. As soon as Terry Venables was named as the new England manager, he received a phone call from his close friend Ron Atkinson.

"Carlton," said Atkinson. "You'll never play for England again."

"He knew what Venables was like," Palmer told me. "He knew that he was well in with the London media and that because there was always this thing with me and the press it was all over."

He left Sheffield Wednesday at the end of the 1993/94 season to join Leeds United in a £2.6 million move. He played over 100 games for the side before a spell at Southampton and then a period at Nottingham Forest. He has managed both Stockport and Mansfield and now owns a pub and a nightclub in Sheffield.

After the disappointment of missing out on a trip to the World Cup, Palmer refused to watch any of the tournament at all. "In your lifetime, you are sometimes lucky enough to have the opportunity to do some major things like play for big teams and appear in Cup Finals. I knew that

I would never have another opportunity to reach a World Cup, so I went away on holiday that summer. After all that misery of missing out, the last thing I wanted to do was watch it on the telly."

Carlton Palmer is now a regular pundit on the BBC's *Final Score*.

11 ● STAN BOWLES
Denting Pride, the FA Cup and Kid Creole (1973–1976)

"I don't really watch football anymore, to be honest with you, Iain," says Stan Bowles in a nicotine-stained voice. "Watching it always bored me, even back when I was playing!" It seems astonishing at first that someone so talented could have so little interest in the sport where he made his name, but after a while in his company it begins to make sense.

Stan is what you might call a matter-of-fact kind of chap. He's a man who has lived his life harder and faster than most and he has a very philosophical attitude to it all. He regards the spellbinding football that he once played as very much a secondary issue in his life. Ranked far higher than football, among other things, are his friends.

We meet in his sister's pub in Manchester where he is sitting with a group of mates, none of whom are former footballers, TV stars or Page 3 girls and one of whom speaks for the rest when he describes Stan as, "A great guy. When he's with us, he's just one of the lads."

I've lost count of the amount of times I've read articles that have described Bowles as being hard-up, but if he is, he certainly doesn't seem to have let it affect him. He's friendly and accommodating and there's a sparkle in his blue eyes that suggests he's having just as much fun as he ever did. He's still well loved by fans of his former clubs. I met Stan the day before he was named as the greatest ever player for two different teams, Queens Park Rangers and Brentford, in a PFA centenary survey, something only Alan Shearer and Stanley Matthews can match.

You can call Stan a lot of things and in fact, if you were a defender in 1970s, you probably already have, but you certainly can't call him ordinary. It seems that he never did anything by the book and played out his career like a bull in John Lewis, not entirely comfortable with his surroundings and unwilling to go quietly when there's that much china to be smashed.

Stan Bowles was born on Christmas Eve in Manchester in 1948. Ludicrously skilful with a football, he was snapped up by Manchester City as a teenager, but clashed repeatedly with Malcolm Allison and Joe Mercer before eventually being fired and told that he'd never amount to anything. A short spell at Bury followed, but it was at Carlisle where Bowles came into his own. He was the ultimate showman, a gifted play-maker with no concept of nervousness and no respect for big-name opponents. He moved to Loftus Road for an enormous-at-the-time fee of £112,000 to fill the gaping hole left by Rodney Marsh and was more than equal to his skilful predecessor.

Dave Sexton was assembling an impressive collection of players at Queens Park Rangers and in the season of 1975/76, they threatened to cause an almighty upset.

I suppose I'd had a colourful career even before I got to Loftus Road. I got sacked by my first club, Manchester City. My own fault really, I never turned up for training. For some reason Malcolm Allison and Joe Mercer took exception to that! I went to Bury and then I ended up at Carlisle where I got my head together for a bit.

The first time I really hit the headlines wasn't to do with winning anything though. I got in a bit of trouble up at Sunderland in 1973 and, you know, I don't think they've forgiven me for it yet. It was right at the end of the season and Ian Porterfield had just scored their winning goal in the FA Cup Final against Leeds. That was some win as well, because Leeds was a very decent team in them days. Anyway, we had to play them a few days afterwards. They're very proud of their Cup win as you can imagine and they've set this table up on the side of the pitch, right by the halfway line, with the Cup plonked on it for everyone to see.

Well, me and Johnny Hazell, we've had a bit of a bet in the dressing room. Who can knock it off the table first! I picked up the ball and tore across the pitch towards it and bang! I think I fucking dented it! This big noise has gone up and there's people trying to get on the pitch to get me. Fucking hell, we almost caused a riot.

I didn't make it any easier by goading their players throughout the game, asking them, "How the fuck did you beat Leeds?" and then to make matters worse I went and scored two goals. The chairman had to come down to the dressing room at half-time 'cos he didn't want us to go back out there again, it was chaos. We were told not to go out in the evening after the game either, just in case. They made us stay in the hotel. They're a fiery bunch those Mackems, ain't they? It was only meant to be a joke. Mind you, I've haven't been back to Sunderland since. Fucking hell, I ain't that silly. Only needs one old bloke to say, "I remember you, Bowles," doesn't it? Nah, I'm alright where I am!

I loved it at QPR. At that time I was flying, you know what I mean? All the way through the 1975/76 season, I felt on top of the world. I really enjoyed my football. Well, I had to, didn't I? It was a bit of a release from the rest of the week, getting chased by gangsters, bookies and bailiffs!

We had a good team as well. John Hollins, David Webb, Frank

McLintock. It was a golden age for those fans, best team they ever had. Dave Sexton had put us together well. Dave was a nice guy, we became good friends years later, but I didn't understand him at first. I'd come out for training and there'd be cones everywhere. I'd think, "Oh, fuck this." Later, when I came round to him, and it took quite a while, don't get me wrong, he was alright. He was a shy man, not too good at handling people like me. I didn't make it easy for him though. I used to take things onboard, but not tell anybody. Still, like I say, I became good friends with him after that.

The rest of the team couldn't understand why I was so calm all the time. You've gotta remember that all these players, Big Frank, Johnny Hollins, they've all won stuff, but they were all so nervous before a game. Frank had won the double with Arsenal, but it didn't help at all. It was the same when I went to Forest. All these players there who'd won the European Cup and they was all fucking nervous. Fucking hell, what can the crowd do to you? They can't do fuck all, can they?

No one could understand how I could just stroll into the dressing room ten minutes before kick-off, stick me kit on and go out and play. The thing was, every game was just a Sunday morning kickaround for me. Put your kit on and off you go. I've always been like that; I never got nervous. When people are chasing you for gambling debts it puts things in perspective, know what I mean? That 90 minutes was a relief!

Where was I before the game? I was in the betting shop! It's the truth! It's no secret at all, there was a betting shop just down the road and I used to pop in there. I used to get the fans coming up to me saying, "Aren't you playing today, Stan?" and I'd be going, "'Course I am. I've got a few minutes left, haven't I?"

Had to stop in the end. Players started moaning about it and someone shopped me to Dave. He said, "You've got to stop this, Stan." I suppose you wouldn't get that with Cristiano Ronaldo, would you? It never stopped my career, the betting. It never got in the way of anything. I was an unlucky c**t, but there you go, it didn't affect my game. It's just one of those things, isn't it? I know the rules. You either win or you lose, don't you?

I had a good bet on us to win the league at the start of the season, 33/1 for the title. I really thought that was going to come in for me. We beat Liverpool on the opening day of the season at Loftus Road and that didn't happen too often. We were top of the table in October after putting five past Everton! With five games to go we was 5/1 on. I've never seen Queens Park Rangers at 5/1 on to win anything. You'll never see that again! We knew it was a good side. We went to Germany and beat all the top teams over there that pre-season and we had a bit of feeling. Even Dave said, "Look, we can win this league, you know."

Yeah, I always look back on that season and think that, really, we should have won the title. We were definitely the most entertaining side anyway. When we played midweek games, you'd see 20 managers up in the stands watching, 'cos they knew something would happen. We didn't take the prospect of winning it too seriously at first, but towards the end of the season there was a feeling amongst the players that we could actually do it.

I still don't know how we lost it. We had some silly draws against teams like Sheffield United and Derby, that didn't help. We had a miserable Christmas as well. But we never lost at home all season. That'll never happen at QPR again either! From our last nine games we won eight of them and lost just once away at Norwich. We were one point clear and then we had two weeks to wait for it all to end. Liverpool were off playing in Europe and they couldn't play their last game till afterwards. We were basically champions for two weeks and then they came back. They had to beat Wolves who needed a win to survive. Twelve minutes left and Wolves were winning 1–0. But then Liverpool hit three goals in the closing stages and that was that.

People say it was unfair that we had to do our games and then they could come back knowing what they had to do, but what difference does it make, eh? I watched the game at the BBC studios, funnily enough, with Gerry Francis. I watched up until the equaliser and that was it. It would have been over even with a draw because of the goal difference. I said to Gerry, "They'll fucking murder 'em now," then I went down the pub and got drunk.

We did alright in Europe the next season, but it wasn't the same. The lads were getting older. That was the end of the story basically. We never got that close again and I never felt the same way about football.

It certainly didn't feel the same when I moved to Nottingham Forest. I didn't get on with Brian Clough at all. I just wasn't sure about him.

When I joined he said to me, "You bloody cockneys are all the same."

I said, "I'm not a cockney, I'm from fucking Manchester."

So that was us off on the wrong foot straightaway. He thought he was Mr Smartarse, didn't he? I wanted to prove that I was the cleverest so I told him that I had all these O-levels and A-levels. That was alright until he found out I was bullshitting and then he lost his temper with me again.

I was only there 11 months; I hated it. Clough must have had something for him to win all those trophies, but I certainly don't know what it was. He never did any coaching for starters. It's true. It was the little Scotsman, Jimmy Gordon, he did all the training. Clough and Peter Taylor just used to walk down the Trent with the fucking dogs. That was it. A lot of those players like Martin O'Neill they liked him, but I didn't.

Charlie George came down on loan for a bit and he was the same as me. Cloughie had a go at him in the dressing room and he retaliated.

Clough said, "When I tell you to play centre-forward, young man, I want you to play centre-forward."

Charlie said, "Why don't you fuck off, you northern c**t?"

He got sent back after that! All the other players, Trevor Francis, all of that, they're all looking at the floor. They don't want a confrontation. Fuck him, he's only a person, isn't he? And these are players who've won everything. I think that's one of the things that strengthened us at QPR. We were treated like adults.

I suppose it was a bit of a golden era for football in general, the 1970s. There were so many good players about. Every team had a couple of stars. There was Frank Worthington, Tony Currie. He was great, Currie. When I played with him I thought, "Fucking hell, I didn't know he was this good." Alan Hudson, Charlie George, all great players. It was just one of those eras, where quality players appear all over the place.

Football was a bit different back then. You didn't get the pitches you get now. Loftus Road was actually built on a tip, you know. If it rained for an hour and a half before the game, you'd have to call it off. We had a lot of games called off.

I had a lot of people who wanted to get stuck into me, as well. Ronny Harris at Chelsea, he was one. I used to get him booked as soon as I could. I used to wind him up from the start and he'd always bite. That would put him one foul away from a red card.

I'd say, "Now look, you've gone and done it again, ain't cha?"

That would wind him up even more! We didn't lose many games

against Chelsea when I was there, funnily enough. Scared? Nah, I was a protected species at Shepherds Bush! If anyone wanted me, they had to go through my gang first. My father always taught me, "Safety in numbers." Good lesson to learn, that.

It's not just the football that was different then. People say that our generation would struggle with the press nowadays, but I used to get followed about by reporters all the time.

I used to say to them, "Follow me round all you want, pal, I'm off to the dog tracks. If you want to fucking join me, you're more than welcome."

It worked; they stopped following me about then.

I spent all my time at the race track in those days. I used to get journalists trying to do stories on me with women, but I didn't have time for it back then. Mind you, I've had three wives since then! They always tried to do celebrity stories on me as well, but I didn't go for that lifestyle.

That said, I knew Phil Lynott from Manchester, and I got back in contact with him when I was at Loftus Road. He'd moved to London and we met up again. I used to have a share in a wine bar in Notting Hill and Phil opened it for us.

I said, "How much do you want?"

He said, "I don't want anything. Well, actually, I'll do it for a bottle of Jack Daniels."

Do you remember Kid Creole and the Coconuts? They were there that night and Phil couldn't stand them. He wound up throwing the empty bottle and it hit the lead singer right on the fucking head! These were my mates though. I'd known Phillip for a long time. He was normal like me. Well, nearly normal anyway. Great guy, he was.

I never moved in other circles though, just with my mates. I kept in contact with my old friends. I've always been the same. People are my mates, whether they're in football or out, it's never bothered me. I didn't go for trendy nightclubs or anything like that. My only other brush with celebrities happened on a TV show and even now, I still get people asking me about it. They all want to know about *Superstars*!

I was at QPR when I did it. It was a big TV programme at the time, kind of like a celebrity sports day, wasn't it? Anyway, to me it was just a fucking joke. The army organised it over at Aldershot and they had me as the footballer against James Hunt, the racing driver, and this hurdler and some other well-known names of the time. They had us in the gym doing weights first of all and I was like, "No, no, no, I can't do that, mate. Got a bad back". You can't detect a back injury, can you? I said, "Nah, not for me." Got away with it, but those soldiers were disgusted with me.

I had even worse luck in the rowing, I fucking capsized! That gave everyone a laugh. I was a bit too hungover for the swimming, so that didn't go well. Then it was down to the target shooting round. I'm standing there with this gun and this soldier, he's got medals all over him, he's standing in front of me, next to this table, and he says to me, "I can kill a man from 100 yards."

I nodded, accidentally pulled the trigger and blew the fucking table in half! That must have convinced him that I could kill a man from a lot closer, 'cos he stood behind me after that! I didn't hit the target once. I still hold the record for the lowest points ever.

If I played professional football now, I don't think I'd get away with anything like that. I'd never swap what I had for what they've got now though. Like I told you, I don't even watch football now. I never liked watching it; I was just reasonably good at it.

But I had a good career. Some people think I only played for QPR, but I played for 17 years. I played for England. I only played five times, but I still did it. It was the Scotland game that ended it for me. Joe Mercer took me off and I walked out. He didn't like that. They never used to ban you from England, but once you were out, you were out. Didn't bother me though, I was happier playing for QPR than I was playing for them. You gotta remember when I was flying, I was taking the piss out of the players I was playing with and they didn't like that at England. They went a bit frosty. It didn't bother me. I got on well with Mick Channon. He was my room-mate; still my mate to this day.

People have these ideas about me but I laughed every day when I was playing football, I really did. The game's changed now, it's sad. I used to stand outside Loftus Road for an hour and a half signing autographs after a match. What do they do now? They get in their cars and drive off after the game, don't they? There's good players out there, but I've been to Arsenal with Charlie George and I've seen 'em just driving off without a care in the world. They might give a wave, but that's all they give. Back in the '70s, I used to drink with the QPR fans after the game in a pub right next to the betting shop. That was against the rules as well. We had this rule book, pages of things you couldn't do, and you were supposed to only drink outside a two mile radius of the stadium.

When Dave Sexton found out he said, "You can't keep doing that."

I said, "Look, when I finish the game, that's it. I'm finished. I do what I want."

Nah, I wouldn't change what I've achieved for anything. I played for England. Malcolm Allison and Joe Mercer told me I'd never play football again, but I done it. I done what they said I wouldn't do.

Bowles left QPR for Nottingham Forest, but didn't hang around for long. A move to Leyton Orient beckoned and then, in 1981, there was a final stint at Brentford with his former nemesis Ron Harris.

Bowles admits he lost much of his enthusiasm for football after leaving QPR. He turned down a chance to win a European Cup medal with Nottingham Forest when he clashed with Brian Clough before the game and walked out. Clough couldn't believe that the row was about Bowles' non-selection for his friend's testimonial. But then Bowles was rarely anything less than unbelievable. These days, he wouldn't have made it past a Premier League youth team. Not because he was a bad player but because of his attitude. On the pitch he would be a match for most in the top flight. Off it, he simply wouldn't have accepted the constricting rules and codes of today's football. It's football's loss, but it makes you wonder how many other mavericks we've missed out on in the last 20 years.

Not that Bowles will be too concerned though. He readily admits that he wouldn't be able to survive these days and would be far happier if the polished entertainment served up today reverted back to the rough and ready fare of yesteryear.

"We used to be able to say anything to referees and they'd take it in the spirit it was intended, not like this lot today," he told me. "I had this one ref and I said to him, 'What would you do if I called you a c**t, referee?'

"He says, 'I'd have to send you off, Stan.'

"I said, 'What about if I just thought you were a c**t?'

"'Well,' he says, 'I wouldn't be able to do anything about that.'

"'Good,' I said, ''cos I think you're a c**t.'"

Stan Bowles' *The Autobiography* was published in 1996 by Orion Books. Stan is also available for after-dinner work at www.soccerspeaker.com.

12 ● FRANK McAVENNIE
Upton Park, Stringfellow's and a Title Race (1986)

He's been broke, he's been imprisoned and he's been lampooned, but it seems that nothing can take the sparkle from Frank McAvennie's eyes. He bounds out of his car at Newcastle Central to greet me, looking for all the world like an over-excited golden retriever. If he had a tail to wag, it would have wiped out the two old ladies trying to cross the road behind him.

He invites me to hop in and we set off to a restaurant in town owned by a friend of his. It is immediately apparent that McAvennie drives like he lives, laughing all the way and with only the faintest regard for his own safety.

"You're interviewing Frank?" chuckles the owner when we arrive. "I hope he doesn't clam up on you, he's a very shy lad, is Frankie! He might just vanish into his shell."

This is clearly not the case. After five minutes in his company, I'm fairly convinced that he hasn't seen the inside of his shell in years. Every story he tells is pre-empted by a hearty laugh and he swings and shuffles excitedly in his chair as he speaks.

For all of the lows that McAvennie has encountered in life, you get the impression that the highs have more than made up for it. He seems happy and settled in the north-east now, but that doesn't mean that he regrets a single night of his past. He mentions one evening in particular, when he was in Stringfellow's with the eponymous owner and a fairly well known Page 3 girl of the time.

"Ah," I smiled wistfully. "I used to have pictures of her hidden in my bedroom when I was 10."

"Did you?" he laughs. "I used to have her hidden in my bedroom when you were 10!"

Frank and I, it has to be said, have lived very different lives.

Frank McAvennie was born in Glasgow in 1959 and was a precocious talent as a youngster. He joined St Mirren in 1980 and started as he was to go on, scoring twice in his first competitive game against Airdrie. In his first full season, 1981/82, he won the Scottish Young Player of the Year award and broke into the under 21 national side.

By the mid-eighties he was a hot property and St Mirren began to receive interest from England. For a while he seemed certain to join David Pleat at Luton Town, but then John Lyall saw his chance to take the young Scotsman to West Ham.

The Hammers weren't exactly perennial League challengers, but in the 1985/86 season something in the team clicked and they started to string wins together. The traditional powerhouses of that period, Liverpool and Everton, suddenly had to look over their shoulders. The Football League title was going to go right down to the wire.

Moving to West Ham was a huge surprise to me because I was supposed to be signing for Luton! I didn't know anything about West Ham's interest. David Pleat had sounded us out, and me and the St Mirren delegation had gone down to Kenilworth Road to finalise it all. It was all set up, but when I got there their chairman, Thatcher's mate David Evans, this big heavy guy, slaps me on the back of the head and he says in this booming voice, "Welcome to Luton, Macca!"

I thought, "Who the hell are you?" I mean, who slaps people on the back of the head the first time they meet them? I looked at my agent and that was that. I told them I'd give them my decision in the morning, but I had no intention of joining them after that. As I walked out, my manager said that West Ham were interested as well. This was news to me. It turned out St Mirren had given Luton first refusal, but the thing was that Luton had paid for us to come down, they'd paid for flights and hotels and all that, so it was going to be a bit embarrassing to call it all off.

Anyway, at half past one in the morning on that same day, I met their manager, John Lyall, at Toddington service station. It was a bit cloak and dagger, but it was good fun driving through the car park in the middle of the night! We sat down in this little canteen and started speaking. He told me all about the club and his plans, but he was always going to get me to sign. I was too tired to say no!

I'd never been away from Glasgow and I was so excited to be signing for West Ham. Everyone had heard of the club. Even a Scotsman like me knew that West Ham had won the World Cup for England in 1966. To have a chance to emulate people like Brooking, Hurst and Peters, och, it was great. I was looking forward to it.

It didn't go too well from the start though. In fact, pre-season was pretty awful, to tell you the truth. John bought me to play behind the strikers, this position that the foreign coaches are supposed to have invented. Nonsense, we done it years ago. Lyall was so far ahead of his time. He brought me in against Orient and it didn't work.

At half-time the door got kicked in and this big guy come in shouting, "You're rubbish, you're fucking rubbish!"

I thought "God, the directors are taking it a bit serious, aren't they?"

It turned out John had got one of the supporters to tell us what he thought of our performance!

Early on in the season Paul Goddard picked up a nasty injury and I was pushed up to partner Tony Cottee. I never looked back after that. My only trouble was that I found it difficult to settle in London. My Scottish accent was so strong that every time I shouted for the ball in training, the lads thought I wanted to fight them! I had to start to speak slower to give them a chance to understand me. The biggest problem though was the loneliness. After all the excitement of moving to the capital, it turned out that I didn't actually like London at all when I arrived. It's a big city and I didn't know anyone. I was stuck miles out in East London and I was bored and homesick. I asked John Lyall if I could go back to Scotland.

He said, "Look, give it three months, see how it goes and if you still don't like it we'll have another chat."

He must have told some of the boys about our conversation because they organised a big night out to show me round London. We started in Gidea Park where I lived and worked our way through the pubs into the centre. We ended up in Stringfellow's where there was this big party on. It was wall-to-wall celebs and I got introduced to everyone. Mind you, I think I was wearing a tartan suit at the time, so there was never any danger of them forgetting about me!

Aye, it's fair to say that I thoroughly enjoyed myself that night. Once I was introduced to London, that was me. I was settled. People knew me and it wasn't a lonely place anymore. It was strange though, because there was barely any TV coverage of football then, so I was top of the goal-scoring charts and nobody knew who I was. People in Stringfellow's knew, but outside of that nobody had a clue.

Then I went and did an interview on *Wogan* one Friday night and 18 million people saw me. That was it; my life was never going to be the same again. I was in Stringfellow's with a girlfriend the night after when I got my first sign that things had changed. I was getting pissed and having a laugh when this girl who worked at the club, Margo, she came over to me. She was a great girl, Margo, the resident photographer there. She came over and she said, "Frank, all the press are waiting outside for you."

I was like, "Erm ... why?"

She said, "Something about Wogan?"

So there was this Sheikh there and Peter Stringfellow convinced him to let me use his limo to get home. I said, "Thanks very much!" The bouncers were great; they got me out of the club with a coat over my head and threw me in the back with my girlfriend. The door slammed and we just sat there laughing at it all, scoffing this Sheikh's free drinks. The thing was, the Sheikh thought we lived just around the corner and that his car would be back in no time. I'd just bought a house in Gidea Park! It was hours before he got that limo back!

There was no question of me neglecting my duties. John knew me and how I was and no matter what, I was a professional footballer. I went out and partied but it didn't interfere with my football. I never went out two days before a game, never even thought about it. I did go out after games, of course I did, but you could get away with it back then. No matter where I've been, however I've felt, I've given 110 per cent when I've played, every time.

The team was really close and we were doing as well on the pitch as I was off it. My partnership with Tony Cottee was red hot. I played my first game up front against QPR at home and I remember this big centre-back, Alan McDonald, done Tony a couple of times. He was a bit of a bully, so I waited until he had the ball on the touchline and

I just banged him into the Chicken Run [one of the more brutal parts of West Ham's ground]. He didn't like that, he was getting slapped off all the fans in there; it was brilliant! That's when the supporters started to take to me. Going up the other end and scoring didn't hurt either! I scored two in that game, so the fans were quickly on my side. I always played with a smile on my face and I always gave 110 per cent and they see that from the stands, they know who's trying and who isn't.

I never realised the extent to which they were behind me until an incident in a pub in East London. The ICF, the InterCity Firm, were the big boys at the time and I was in this pub called The Moby Dick. I was in there with a girlfriend, just having a quiet drink and somebody started having a pop at us.

I just thought, "Whatever", but it carried on and carried on and carried on.

I thought "I'm not having this all night", and I says to my girlfriend, "Hold on a minute, I'm just going to the toilet." I figured that he'd follow me in there and I could take him.

So off I went to the loo and I was standing around for ages. Nothing.

I thought, "Oh well, maybe I got that wrong".

I walked out the toilet and there he was, spark out on the floor. Somebody had thumped him. I looked down and there was a small card on his back.

"Congratulations, you've just been done by the ICF," it read.

Heh! Heh! Heh! I looked around and it was like nothing had happened. Everyone just carried on drinking and no one looked at me. Fifty witnesses and none of them saw a thing!

Back to matters on the pitch and, despite a decent start, we began to slip away before Christmas. Big Alvin Martin [a long-standing defender] called a players meeting to sort it all out. Just players, mind, no management or staff were allowed. We got it sorted there and then. We needed to stick to what we were good at and we all needed to get stuck in more. I always defended from the front and I was busting my arse trying to get the ball back. That's why John bought me. He knew I wouldn't give anyone a moment's peace. I was just a pest really! I suppose I was a bit like Craig Bellamy. I didn't give anyone a let-off, I was always snapping at people's ankles.

We had one lad, Neil Orr, another Scotsman. Now, as long as he didn't try and play he was great, if you know what I mean. John had to have a word with him because he kept getting the ball and trying to play 40-yard passes.

John said, "Look, just you give the ball to Devonshire and Ward. They can play, you can't."

I thought it was a bit strong at the time, but I knew what he was saying. He was saying just do your job, tackle, get the ball. No one could do what Neil did. Get it and give it to someone who can play, that's how it works. And it did work. After that meeting we went on a hell of a run. I think we must have gone something like 17 games without a defeat. Incredible.

I think ultimately our biggest fault that year was trying to win everything. We tried to chase the double, but we didn't have a big enough squad. If we'd had more players we could have won every-thing, you know, we were that good. But we only played 16 players that year and we had a lot of games – a lot of games. It was all because of the weather. We played Ipswich on February 6 and then we didn't play another one until March 5 against Manchester United! We didn't have under-soil heating then, so when it snowed, that was it, you just couldn't play football. It wasn't all bad though, I had a lot of good nights out during that period, I can tell you! It meant that we had to squeeze a quarter of the season into one month at the end and at one point we were playing Saturday, Monday, Wednesday.

Was I tired? Och, no! You're joking, aren't you? None of the boys were tired, that's why I can't understand all this fatigue stuff nowadays. I didn't like training anyway and with a programme like that we didn't do any. And we did well, you know. We played some great football that year. My partnership with Tony Cottee was amazing. We were having bets during the games on who could score the best goal! The confidence was bursting out of us. Mind you, it got us in trouble. We played once at Aston Villa and Tony hit one from 30 yards. I knew I had to do something special to get his money, so I lobbed the keeper from close range when I didn't really need to! It went in, but John made some enquiries and found out what we were up to. He fined us both a week's wages! We had a £100 bet and John did us for a grand! Och, it was fun, what a season. I loved Tony, but we were so different. Two sides of the same coin, we used to say. He met me one night in Stringfellow's. Thing is, we met at the door, he left at about the same time that I was just getting started!

I could handle my drink though and I always made sure I could get home. I was always alright that way. I remember sitting and having a discussion with a girl on a balcony in London at 5am. Bizarre. Just sitting there at 5am with all these people walking by who must have been thinking, "What the fuck is he doing?" Aye, London's a strange place. I love it. I just can't live there. I know people, they know me and if I lived there it would just snowball again!

The thing I loved about London most was that I was only a footballer and there were so many major stars down there: Elton John, Rod Stewart and all of that. I'd look at them in nightclubs and think, "Nobody's gonna bother about me." In that respect, it was great. I met Jack Nicholson in Stringfellow's. Jack probably tells everyone how he met me now, ha, ha, ha!

We just got introduced, he was Peter's guest and he was like, "Hey man! You a soccer player?"

He took all the girls that night, I remember that much! All the good-looking girls went over to him! Sometimes I might hit a night out in Los Angeles with Rod Stewart! I went to the opening of Peter's Stringfellow's in New York and the one in LA. Aye, I've travelled, ha, ha, ha! I like Stringfellow's, did you notice?! God, it was good fun.

When I'm down in London now it's incredible, people just come out to you and talk to you about what you did there. It's unbelievable but it's difficult, because I'm very shy ... as you can tell, ha, ha, ha!

I was in the tabloids a lot back then for my private life, but you know what? I'm from Milton in Glasgow. It's a council estate. I go from there and suddenly, I'm in the papers for all this stuff with girls and people come up to me and say, "Oh, that must get to you."

I'm like, "You must be having a fucking laugh, aren't you?"

I know that all the boys I went to school with are thinking, "You lucky bastard!"

I'm getting caught with some of the most beautiful women in Britain and they're all asking if it bothers me? It's just ... God, it never ceases to amaze me!

Och, but we just fell short on the pitch that year. It all came down to the penultimate day. We had to win at The Hawthorns and hope that Liverpool dropped points at Stamford Bridge. If they did that, we could beat Everton in the final game and win the title. We won our game 3–2 and as we left the pitch someone told us that Chelsea had held them 0–0. We were over the moon, bouncing up and down in the dressing room. It was five minutes before John Lyall came in and broke the bad news. Kenny Dalglish had won it in the last few minutes. I've never forgiven Chelsea for that.

I was devastated. We still had to play Everton for second place, but we were crushed. Absolutely crushed. I wish now that we'd managed to lift ourselves, you know, just for the record books to name us runners-up, but you couldn't have motivated us then. I was called up for the Scotland World Cup squad, but it wasn't any consolation. I wanted the title.

Sometimes I wonder how it would be if I was a player now. I don't think I'd be much different. I'd still be the same. People ask me if I feel sorry for modern players and the constant media exposure they get, but bollocks to that. No, I don't. I think they're pampered. Some of them are great lads, but they're forgetting who they are. They moan and moan. I used to love football and I was getting the shit kicked out for me for a grand a week; a hundred grand a week? Christ, you could get anyone to have a kick at me for that money!

No, I don't regret anything at all. I wouldn't swap a single night or a single game. There's no point in changing anything. I am what I am.

West Ham lost their final game of the season to Everton and finished third in the table, four points adrift of champions Liverpool. They never came that close to the title again.

Frank McAvennie left the club for Celtic at the end of the following season.

"I didn't want to leave," insists Frank. "The policy of the club was that they wouldn't pay me another signing-on fee if I put pen to paper on a new deal. It's a short career and I needed to make sure my pension was topped up. I don't think John would have let me go, but he knew that I was a Celtic lad and it was something I had to do."

McAvennie finally got his hands on silverware at Parkhead. In his first season he won the Scottish Premier League and the Scottish Cup, scoring both goals in the 2–1 victory in the Final at Hampden Park. However, his relationship with the London-based model Jenny Blyth meant that he was returning from Glasgow to the capital after every weekend game to spend time with her. Inevitably he moved south, turning down a move to Arsenal in order to return to Upton Park. The Gunners went on to win the title, but McAvennie's West Ham were unable to even come close to the heights of the 1985/86 season.

"I couldn't have gone to Arsenal," he laughed. "That would have been like joining Rangers. I couldn't have done it to the fans."

His last act in a West Ham shirt was to score a hat-trick, but by that point the club had already been relegated and, by his own account, McAvennie had experimented with cocaine during a long-term injury. A spell at Aston Villa, a return to Celtic and periods at Falkirk, Swindon and St Mirren all followed before his retirement.

Unfortunately McAvennie hit the headlines again when he spent a month on remand in Durham Prison after being charged with drug offences, a charge of which he was eventually cleared. This part of his story is better recounted in his fantastic autobiography, details of which are listed below.

McAvennie insists that trophies and medals are not the be all and end all of modern football.

"The fans are the most important thing in the game. You can have the glory and all that, but it just gives me so much pleasure when someone comes up and talks to me about West Ham or Celtic. Just to see what it means to so many people. It beats everything. That's what it's all about for me."

Frank McAvennie's autobiography, *Scoring – An Expert's Guide*, is available from Canongate Books.

13 ● ALAN KENNEDY
No Pressure, Al (1984)

Sometimes, with interviews, you're never entirely sure if you've got anything really special until you play the tape back afterwards. You might think that you've spent the afternoon skilfully filleting your subject with a series of searching questions, when all you've really done is boorishly talk over him. Occasionally, you might believe that you've allowed your target to reveal more by just letting him chunter away uninterrupted, but that belief is usually quashed when you listen back to two hours of unprintable, disjointed waffle.

I knew that Alan Kennedy's chapter was going to be good before I'd even pressed the stop button. The Liverpool legend is precise, knowledgeable and builds the tension so well that, when he was describing the final moments of this game I found myself so far onto the edge of my seat that I was almost in his lap. The encouraging sight of our waiter spending 15 minutes wiping the table behind Kennedy as his story reached its climax was rather nice as well.

Many footballers are unable to remember anything more than the mundane details of the most exciting games of all time, but Kennedy is the absolute opposite. I couldn't have been given more information if I'd had him hypnotised by a stage magician. Every sound, every touch, every feeling of that game in Rome was hauled up for my delectation.

He is polite, softly-spoken and modest of his stellar achievements. He puts his polished performances in a Liverpool shirt down to the fact that he was always aware that the club had the finances to replace him at any time.

He was born in Sunderland in 1954, and came through the ranks at Newcastle as a measured, cultured left-back. Brought to Anfield by Bob Paisley as a replacement for the Anfield folk hero Joey Jones, he admitted that the Welshman's boots were going to be difficult to fill. He needn't have worried. Within a handful of seasons Kennedy had added his own name to the history books by scoring the winning goal against Real Madrid in the 1981 European Cup Final in Paris. He struck home with just nine minutes left on the clock, winning the competition for Liverpool for the third time.

He further endeared himself to the fans by crashing home another important goal in the League Cup Final of 1983, against Manchester United at Wembley. The player known as Barney Rubble on the terraces was quickly gaining a reputation for being the right man at the right time.

Three years after victory in Paris, Liverpool made it to the European Cup Final once again. This time the opposition was AS Roma and, as can sometimes happen, the game was played at their home stadium, the Stadio Olimpico. Surely Kennedy couldn't do it again?

There's a lot of ways you can prepare for a European Cup Final, but I liked Joe Fagan's method the best. Our season ended two weeks before the big game in Rome and Joe decided to take us to Israel for a bit of a break. We'd been there before and it's a wonderful place. However, when we got there the Italian press were waiting for us. We had to do a deal with them and meet them on the beach for lots of pictures and interviews before they'd leave us alone. After they went, we were much more relaxed, but the Italians must have loved it. "Look at the English," they must have laughed. "They're all out drinking!"

We did do a bit of light training while we were there, but we had such a good time afterwards. We knew we had a job to do when we played Roma, but this was what we needed at the end of a long season, a chance to relax and socialise. We had a lot of jokers in that team and we had a lot of laughs in Israel. When we returned to England a few days later, the work began in earnest.

We went out to Italy on the Monday before the match on Wednesday night. We didn't really get a chance to see much of Rome, we were so busy focusing on the game, but we could sense the atmosphere building up around us. The fans would come into the hotel and talk to us, ask us how we were doing, and it felt like the day before a carnival. We were all in really good spirits.

You're always apprehensive before a big game though. I wouldn't say nervous, because a lot of teams feared Liverpool at the time, but this was going to be tough. The game was actually being played at Roma's home stadium, so we knew we had to be at our best to nullify them. There was going to be 85,000 people there and the majority of them were supporting Roma.

I think the fact that we'd been through this before in Paris in 1981 helped a lot, but an awful lot of those players had gone. Ray Clemence, David Johnson, Terry McDermott, Jimmy Case, Ray Kennedy had all left and been replaced by Ian Rush, Stevie Nicol, Ronnie Whelan, Mark Lawrenson and, of course, Bruce Grobbelaar. Apart from Bruce though, they were all experienced players.

When you look back at that team, it was probably one of the strongest sides the club has ever had. That back five of me, Phil Neal, Alan Hansen, Lawrenson and Grobbelaar, we knew where we all were, what we were supposed to be doing and we felt like a unit. We were well drilled.

The night before the game we got together and played cards. Everyone liked a game of cards. There was no bad behaviour though. The manager always said, "Get off to bed nice and early, get your sleep now."

I was rooming with Alan Hansen and he was a good sleeper. It didn't matter what the circumstances were, he'd be out like a light. In some ways he was the perfect room-mate, but I have to tell you, he was the laziest person I've ever shared with. I had seven years with him and I can only remember him getting up and making me a cup of tea on one occasion! It was away at Norwich City and I couldn't believe my eyes when I woke up and saw him up and about. It was always me who made the tea, but he'd got up and put the kettle on. I couldn't figure it out until I remembered it was my birthday! That's the only time he ever did it.

It was difficult being told when to go to sleep, but we all did it. We were just so used to it by then. The problem was that we all knew that the women, our wives and girlfriends, were on the floor above us and we wanted to, you know, say goodnight! Did anything happen? No, I don't think so! In all seriousness, we were too professional. Anyway, we had guards throughout the hotel making sure that nothing disrupted our sleep, not even them.

We didn't realise quite how many people would be watching and listening at that time, but we had a feeling it was going to be very big. It was a bit frustrating to be honest, all you wanted to do was get out there and play the game, but you couldn't. You had to keep living by this schedule, being told what to do, what to eat and when to eat it. I just wanted to play.

There were a lot of superstitions in our team. I had to be the third out or the third from last out and I really don't know why. Others had things like pants on first, left sock on first. It was a weird sight seeing everyone get ready in that dressing room. The strangest one was Bruce. He couldn't leave the dressing room until he'd kicked the ball at the light switch and turned it off. He did it before every game and I have to say, when it's gone five to three and there's only ten players on the pitch, it does worry you! You'd be standing around waiting and getting nervous and then all of a sudden Bruce would run out shouting, "I've done it!" and you knew it was going to be alright.

It sounds silly, all these superstitions, but you have to get your preparation right. Bruce was really strange though, I think at one point he got into war-paint in a big way. We used to call him Jungleman. He'd sit there in the corner eating this weird South African dried meat that looked like wood shavings. It was horrible stuff, like liquorice. He had curious ways, Bruce, but what a goalkeeper he was.

Mind you, he didn't like to take the blame for anything. He made a terrible mistake in a game once, charging out recklessly, and we conceded a goal. He immediately turned and started berating me. "That's your fault," he shouted.

"Get away," I said. "How is it my fault? It was your mistake."

"I know it was my mistake, but it was your fault. You shouldn't have let him get the cross in."

"Oh right ... I see." I said. "I won't let it happen again, eh?" You couldn't win with Bruce.

Joe Fagan was a good manager and he treated his players like men, which was important. He was a man of substance. Bob Paisley was a quiet man who didn't like shouting at players, but when Joe said something forcefully, you'd better believe it. There were eruptions otherwise. He was a strong man, a strong character and he believed in strong values. He was trying to educate us and some of us needed it. When you're only 23 you don't really know what Liverpool Football Club is all about and he believed very strongly in everything the club stood for. Make no mistake, when he spoke, you listened.

Joe didn't over-emphasise what we had to do that night. He didn't need to; it was drilled into us for months beforehand. All the coaching staff, Ronnie Moran particularly, just kept reminding you of your duties. It was one consistent message and we didn't need anything different, even ten minutes before a European Cup Final.

We were like a coiled spring when we left the dressing room. We trooped out of the dressing room and lined up next to the Italians in the tunnel, everyone staring forward and thinking about what they had to do. And then the weirdest thing happened. David Hodgson and Craig Johnston started it, I think. From nowhere they just started singing this Chris Rea song, *I Don't Know What It Is, But I Love It*. One by one, we all started joining in and before anyone knew what was going on, we were all standing there blasting it out down the tunnel. You've got Roma lined up next to us, all these magnificent looking Italians and Brazilians with sculpted hair, looking at us going, "What the hell are they doing?" It was fantastic, we were dancing about as we came out the tunnel and they didn't know what was going on!

We were brilliant when that game kicked off. We kept possession and we controlled the game really well. It was strange because it felt like the crowd were miles away. The Stadio Olimpico is a very open stadium, so it was an odd atmosphere out there. We knew where the Liverpool fans were, but it was like a blur. Joe had said in his pre-match talk, in every pre-match talk, keep the ball, don't give it away. And we did.

And then Phil Neal put us ahead. Phil always, always, always followed the path of the ball once a move was in motion. We had this kind of Total Football thing about us sometimes where defenders could end up front if they followed moves through and it paid off. The ball went to the far post and Ronnie Whelan headed it towards the goal. A Roma defender went in to clear it, but only succeeded in blasting his own goalkeeper in the face. The ball rebounded back and there was Phil to finish it. He had limitless energy, but we were told all the time, if you find yourself in an advanced position, take it on. Become a striker. That's what he did and that's why he scored.

Bruce made some good saves in the first half and the game seemed to pass quickly. Once we scored that goal it settled us right down and as the break approached, we were feeling very, very confident about the way it was going. Then, just before the interval, a cross came in from Phil's side and their striker, Roberto Pruzzo, managed to get above Lawrenson and head it into the top corner. It was a brilliant header, it has to be said. Maybe we could have defended it better, but the lad did well. It was a bad time to concede a goal, a minute before halftime.

Our heads went down and I think they could see it. Joe wasn't happy at the break, but the response was good. The coaches weren't negative at all. We were all disappointed, but Joe just said, "Come on, let's get around each other, forget about the goal and up the tempo a bit."

There were no recriminations in the dressing room. How can you have a go at two of the finest centre-backs and one of the best right-backs ever? It was nothing to do with me, obviously! No, no one was bellowing or shouting, we were just disappointed. We felt like we'd let ourselves down.

The second half was a lot tighter. The more the game went on, the more the fear factor kicked in. Neither team wanted to concede and no one wanted to push forward. Extra-time got closer and closer and no one looked likely to break through. It was a hot, humid night and we were beginning to tire out there.

By the time the whistle had gone and we were in extra-time, it was horrible. Even though I felt that we were stronger, we were all frightened of making a mistake, of doing anything silly that would give away a goal. There were lots of simple balls, lots of back-passes to the goalkeeper. The pace of the game had slowed right down and I think we all knew where it was heading.

The final whistle blew and it was time for penalties. This was, I think, only the second ever penalty shoot-out, so no one really knew what to expect. Deep down we thought if it went to that then we probably had the stronger calibre of player. We've come to their ground where they play week in and week out and it's 1–1. You're just hoping that you have the strength of character to pull through. The fans had helped us as much as they could, singing their hearts out throughout the game. When the match was on a knife-edge, we needed them most and they were there.

I don't think there was very much preparation for that penalty shoot-out at all. Joe just walked around looking at people and sizing them up. I don't know what he said to anyone else, but he looked at me and, these were his exact words, he said, "Are you alright?"

I didn't know what he was getting at, I just thought it was an innocent enquiry.

"'Course I'm alright," I said. "No problem."

I didn't realise he was essentially asking if I wanted to take a penalty. It was only a few minutes later when he was giving the names out and I heard Kennedy being called that I realised what had happened. I didn't know which penalty I was taking, where I was taking it, anything at all. There was a bit of confusion because no one had really thought about it. We didn't even know where to stand. It turned out that I had to take the fifth penalty and I didn't know if that was good or bad. We'd practised them a week before and we were absolutely pathetic. The manager had to call an end to it because we were so bad!

Why did Steve Nicol take the first one? Looking back I can't figure it out. He was the youngest member of the team. Was he just being brave? Was he actually that confident? I don't know. I asked him afterwards and all he said was that he just really wanted to take one, he just wanted to get it all over with. Unfortunately, he missed, hitting it high over the bar. I was just standing there on the halfway line thinking, "God, what's going to happen next?"

They scored their first one and then Phil Neal went up and put his away, nice and calmly. Then everything was turned upside down again when Bruno Conti stepped up and blasted the ball over the top. I couldn't believe he missed because he was a wonderful player. He was left-footed as well, and as a fellow lefty, I always think there's a certain confidence about our breed when we take penalties. But there it was, 1–1 after two penalties each.

Our captain, Graeme Souness, stepped up and put a rocket into the top corner, but then Ubaldo Righetti sent Bruce the wrong way and made it 2–2.

Unsurprisingly Ian Rush didn't have any problems at all, sliding it slowly into the bottom corner. 3–2.

Francesco Graziani was up next, but Bruce had a bit of a surprise for him. Actually, it was a bit of a surprise to everybody when he stood there, wobbling his legs about all over the place. It turned out Joe Fagan and said to him, "Try and put 'em off. Do anything, anything you like." So Bruce started biting the net, wobbling about and bouncing backwards and forwards. Graziani ran forward and fired it high at the goal, but just too high. It clipped the top of the bar and went over. Bruce went bananas, sprinting round in circles and waving his arms about. But I stayed very quiet. It was my go next and I suddenly realised that I could win the European Cup for Liverpool if I scored.

As I walked up to the spot, I thought about my friends and family. I just wanted to make them proud of me; I didn't want to let anyone down. It took forever to get to that penalty area and by the time I got there I was thinking about *Star Trek*. Can you believe that? Millions of people watching and all I can think is, "Beam me up, Scotty. Please get me out of this situation, I'll do anything to get out of this." My legs are like jelly and I'm panicking, thinking, "Please, just hit the target, please just hit the target."

Putting the ball down was a big thing for me. I'm thinking, "Don't look at the keeper, don't look at where you're going to put it." When I walked back for my run-up, not even daring to turn around, I can remember seeing a couple of team-mates hiding their faces, unable to watch. The pressure was building up so much and I can't tell you just how much I didn't want to be there.

I ran up and opened my body up at the last second. I wanted to do what John Aldridge went on to do so well with his spot-kicks, feint and trick the keeper. As I connected with the ball all these flash-lights went off behind the goal and still the only thing in my mind was, "I don't want to be here".

It went very central. The ball would have been a comfortable height for the keeper had he gone the right way. Fortunately he didn't!

I ran. I just ran and jumped and had my hands in the air and then, as I approached my team-mates, I did this silly two-footed jump in front of all of them. It was the worst, most ridiculous thing I've ever done in my life. I can't even look at it on video now! In my defence,

I just didn't know what to do. Neither did they. Some ran to me, some ran to the bench, it was bedlam. I was just jumping. What was I thinking? What a night. What a feeling it was to lift that trophy. What a disappointment it was when we got the medals! I remember them; they were in a little red box, this tiny medal the size of a 10p. We all just looked at them and went, "Oh ... is that it?"

It didn't matter though, it just made us want to go on and win another one! After we left the stadium we went to this villa that someone hired out that looked out over the city and we all headed there for the celebrations. Lots of drink, lots of food, lots of entertainment. The wives were there and it was just an amazing night. We celebrated until the small hours.

Football was our job and it always has been. We'd had a job to do, we'd done the job and it made us feel great. But the fact is that after it all finished, we were there with our families and our friends and they were proud of us. That was the most important thing.

Alan Kennedy played just one more season for Liverpool after the triumph in Rome. Joe Fagan retired at the end of the 1984/85 season and his successor, Kenny Dalglish, preferred the young Irish defender Jim Beglin. After seven years at the club, Kennedy was transferred to Sunderland. "I was disappointed that I didn't stay, but the memories for that club will last forever. I can remember something of every game I ever played for them in. It was a great era, but all good things come to an end."

He made over 50 appearances for his hometown club before playing out his career in the most nomadic of styles by turning out for Swedish and Belgian sides as well as a host of non-league teams in England. He now hosts a radio show for Century FM in the north-west, writes a number of columns and is an accomplished after-dinner speaker.

Twenty-four years after taking that final penalty in the Stadio Olimpico, Kennedy found himself in Istanbul to report on a new generation of Liverpool players battling for a fifth European Cup.

"That game was the best performance I've ever seen, better even than anything from our era. I was in the stadium to cover the game, but at half-time I just didn't know what to say. I had a press pass and I walked down to the pitch to do my piece. I talked for a while about damage limitation and then all the players started to re-emerge. I walked back up to my seat and a few Liverpool fans asked me where I'd been.

"'I've just been down having a word with Rafa,' I dead-panned. 'I've told him to stick Hamman on to neutralise Kaka and get Alonso and Gerrard back in the game.'

"Of course, 30 seconds later Hamman's come on and everyone's looking at me in awe. When the first one went in everyone congratulated me. The second one got me hugged and when the third one came in I was being lifted in the air! I thought it was best to milk it as far as I could."

Alan Kennedy is available as an after-dinner speaker at www.soccerspeaker.com.

14 ● TONY WOODCOCK & VIV ANDERSON
Old Big 'Ead (1975–1984)

In the rejected first draft of the Twelve Labours of Hercules, the Greek hero repeatedly overcomes insurmountable odds before giving up on his final task, arranging an interview with Tony Woodcock and Viv Anderson. Firm friends as players at Nottingham Forest, the pair have stayed close outside of the game and are now in business together acting as respected sports consultants in the Middle East. It is a measure of their success in this field that they are so incredibly difficult to tie down.

With the demands of their time so intense, it took me three months to track them to venues as diverse as the Rutland Hotel in Nottingham, Heathrow Terminal One and a gastro-pub in Altrincham for conversations before suddenly realising that I had more than enough information for a completely separate book, let alone just a single chapter.

The pair of them are more than worth the wait. Woodcock and Anderson are like a vintage footballing version of Ant & Dec. They finish each other's sentences, tee each other up for well-rehearsed gags and are only too happy to get the drinks in while the other one is speaking. With more medals between them than a South American general, they know what they're talking about.

Woodcock is the more assured and considered of the two, pondering deeply before moving into new stories. Anderson is the wrecking ball, laying into the conversation with a suddenly recalled dressing-room episode and then collapsing into a gale of laughter.

They were both shy young squad members at Second Division Nottingham Forest when Brian Clough arrived in 1975. Clough had won the League at unfashionable Derby County in 1972 before a very public falling out with the board saw his acrimonious departure. After a brief spell at Brighton, he replaced Don Revie at Leeds United. His short time at Elland Road was an unmitigated disaster. The players resented his abrasive style and he was paid off after just 44 days.

When he walked through the front door of the City Ground, the club was stagnating in the second flight, or as he put it more succinctly in one of his first interviews, "This football team has one thing going for it right now. Me."

Viv: I don't think I made a good impression on Brian Clough when he first arrived at Nottingham Forest. We played Spurs in an FA Cup tie at the City Ground and I came off with cramp after just ten minutes. After the game, he burst into the dressing room, gave a bit of a speech about taking over and slapped up a team-sheet for the replay that didn't have my name on it. I thought, "Oh no, the writing's on the wall for me here."

Tony: You shouldn't have worried; there were rumours that Clough wanted to sign you when he was at Leeds.

Viv: Really? I didn't know that! As a young lad, I just wanted to stay on the team and impress the new manager. I wasn't too concerned about his reputation; I just wanted to play.

Tony: My first day was the other way round. I'd made a bit of a name for myself, but that season I'd been struggling for form and I was out of the side. When Cloughie arrived he put me back in the squad. I was delighted. Finally we had someone in charge who knew what he was talking about!

Viv: For all the stuff that's written about him now, we didn't actually know too much about his managerial style at the time. We didn't really read the papers.

Tony: We soon found out though. We'd gone down to Bisham Abbey to play Tottenham in the replay and I was excited about being in the frame for a return. The day before the game, we're all having lunch and then he comes over. "Young man," he says. "Young man, here's my room key. In front of the door there's a pair of shoes. I want you to go up there and take the shoes inside the room. At the side of the bed there's some polish and a brush. Give 'em a good polish up because I want to look my best for the game tomorrow." Now, I'm 20 years old. Should I stand up for myself?

"I'm having my lunch, boss," I said, but I'd already finished.

"I might be fucking daft, young man," he said, "but I'm not blind."

So I looked down the table at all the seasoned pros for guidance and nothing came back. Then, finally, one fella called George Lyall looked back at me and nodded, as if I should go. So off I went. I polished those shoes, spat on 'em, put 'em back down and went back downstairs.

Cloughie came over to me. "Young man, you'll go far."

He didn't specify whether it was as a footballer or a butler. Then Jimmy Gordon, the first team coach, comes over and he says, "Don't worry, son. He used to do that to Gordon McQueen at Leeds and he was a good player." So that was our first week of Clough. Viv got dropped and I had to clean his shoes!

Viv: I'd have settled for cleaning the shoes! There wasn't anything to suggest that the club was about to change dramatically. Training sessions were very basic. There was nothing clever about it; it was just simple stuff.

"Keep it on the floor," he said. Even corners were either just short or whipped in at the near post. Clubs today, they've got big dossiers on the opposition, and this, that and the other.

Clough just said, "That's a football, you pass it to a team mate."

Tony: "Get hold of the ball then give it to a red shirt!"

Viv: Ha, ha! Or, "Don't kick it up there. If God wanted football to be played in the air he'd have put grass on clouds."

Tony: It was after the game that he really got you thinking. He'd be sat in the changing room with all of the lads and when you left, if he said, "Young man, you are a credit to the game," you knew you were alright. That was a big thing for me. Not a credit to the club, not a credit to him. A credit to the game. I'd walk out swelling with pride after that.

Viv: During the game it could be a different story though. I sat on the bench sometimes and he'd be verbally abusing certain players, absolutely hammering them for everything. We'd walk in at half-time and I'd think, "Oooh dear, this could be nasty." We'd get into the dressing room and he'd walk up to his victim and say, "Well done, lad. Keep it going!"

I'd be sitting there thinking, "What? You've been calling him a shithouse for 45 minutes!"

He'd be there giving it, "You keep that going, son. You'll do for me" and the fella would go out for the second half on cloud nine! I could never figure him out. If you speak to anyone that played for him, they could never work him out either.

Tony: Expect the unexpected every day; that was the only way to survive. He wasn't scared of anyone. He was such a strong personality; he'd just do what he wanted.

Viv: Larry Lloyd stood up to him once.

Tony: I was thinking about that one the other day, you know? We were coming out of a hotel in Athens after a European game and Larry comes out without his club blazer on. Clough says, "Larry? Where's your blazer?"

He says, "Oh, it's in my case, boss, it's all creased."

Clough says, "£25 fine. Get it out and put it on."

Larry's gone, "But … "

"£50" says Clough.

Larry's said, "Hang on … "

"£75"

"But it's gonna be creased!"

"£100"

And we're all sitting around watching this unfold, so Larry doesn't want to give in and he carries on arguing. But Clough's not going to give in either, so it just keeps going up.

"£125 … £150 … £175."

And it went up and up and up! Finally Larry just gave up and hauled it out of his suitcase.

Viv: You just couldn't win against Cloughie.

Tony: He got Gary Birtles once for not shaving before a game.

"You're not shaved, Birtles," said Clough.

"Sorry, boss," he says. "When I sweat I get all red and it chafes me."

Clough just looks at him and says, "You've got three minutes to shave or you're not playing."

Whoosh, off he goes! Three minutes later he's back with all this tissue paper stuck to his chin!

Viv: There was one incident, quite early on, where the team-sheet had gone up and my name was on it. I never used to go out for a warm-up, I preferred to do my stretches in the bath and get ready that way. So I do my preparation and then I sit there in the dressing room, with my feet up, and start flicking through the programme. He comes in and stares at me.

"Get that kit off," he says as the players walk in.

"What?"

"Get that kit off. See him there," he says pointing at the sub. "I think he'll do a better job than you tonight. Give him your kit."

"You serious?"

"Give him your kit."

So I had to take it all off, give it to him and I wasn't even named as the sub myself! I was a young man so I just had to accept it. If Mr Clough didn't think I was right, then I wasn't right. End of story.

Tony: He was like no other, you know. He kept everyone on their toes. You didn't know what mood he was going to be in from one day to the next. In a bad mood, he was a nightmare. Do you remember that run through a patch of wasteland near the training ground?

Viv: I remember that! We'd just got beat by somebody at home, hadn't we? This stretch of land was 50 yards long and full of nettles. We've turned up for training in tracksuits and he says, "Everyone take their bottoms off."

We're like, "Why?"

He says, "Because I'm the boss."

Tony: The grass back there was about three feet high and filled with nettles and there were old bits of concrete lying about everywhere. At one end of it was a load of trees and he told John McGovern to take us through it. So we'd start pounding through this waste-ground with our ankles going over and through to a bunch of trees with branches whipping us in the face all the way.

Viv: We're all coming through the nettles going, "Yowch! Eee! Ow!" all the way. Million pound footballers stumbling all over each other! We got to the end and went, "What the fuck is going on here?"

Tony: And then back we went the other way.

Viv: He was the manager and what he said went. That was his way of telling us that our performance the weekend before hadn't been acceptable.

Tony: Do you remember Peter Shilton's training session for the European Cup Final?

Viv: Ha, ha, ha! Yes, I do! Peter was really serious about training. He liked his warm-ups and he took it all very seriously. Cloughie's told

175

us that we're going to spend the days leading up to the game playing cards and dominoes and Shilts has gone to have a word.

He says, "Boss, I've got to do some training, I've got to."

He's trying to get out and do some practice all the way up until the morning of the game when Cloughie finally relents.

He gets Jimmy Gordon over and he says, "Take him out and give him some handling practice, will you?" But the only place they could find for space was a traffic island! Jimmy had to go on there and move all the bricks and they did the session there in the middle of the traffic!

My mate's come over for the game and he's said, "I've just seen Peter Shilton diving around on a roundabout!" That was the morning of the Cup Final!

Tony: It was a bit of a shock to the system after leaving the club and finding out what other teams did in training. Well, for you more than me, Viv!

Viv: Ha, ha! Yes, when I moved to Arsenal it was an absolute culture shock! Cloughie had told me when I left, "Grass isn't always greener, you know." He was right with regards to training! Don Howe had just taken over at Highbury and I'll always remember that first training session. We went on a five-mile run and I was so far behind. We didn't do running at Forest, we played five-a-sides all the time. Obviously, we did a bit at pre-season, but I was rubbish at it. Larry Lloyd used to beat me. I couldn't concentrate on it; I just got bored. I was fine on the short stuff, and when it came to a game I could run all day long, but running in training wasn't for me. Anyway, I'm plodding along at the back, some way back, I should say, and I hear this heavy breathing behind me. It's only Don Howe, isn't it? He'd set off long after everyone else and now me and Don are sprinting the last 200 yards and I've got to work to beat a man twice my age! Not the way to make a good first impression!

Tony: It wasn't just training that was different. Clough didn't do big team-talks either. He used to say the hardest thing in football is to keep it simple and he kept his pre-match instructions the same. We had Southampton in the League Cup Final in 1979 and we went into the dressing room at half-time losing 1–0.

Viv: I was suspended for that one! Too many bookings. Never mind, I got to play in a few other finals!

Tony: We've come in thinking that he's going to go into one, but he didn't. He just sat us all down and got us quiet. Then he simply said, "Don't worry, boys. When you go out there for the second half, as soon as you get the ball, just pass it to a red shirt. Don't think about positioning, don't think about making chances, just give it to another red shirt."

Now, we had players who followed their instructions closely and when we came out for the second half, that's all we did. We got the ball; we passed it on. We got the ball again; we passed it on again. Without even thinking about it, we found our natural game and stopped Southampton from getting anywhere near us. We went on to win 3–2.

Viv: He was always very straightforward with what he expected of me. He said, "I'm paying you to defend, with Larry and Kenny and Frank, that's your job. I want you to defend first and foremost and if you can't do that, you're not in my team." I was encouraged to get forward but only when the time was right. My job was to kick the winger just to make sure that he didn't have an easy afternoon. Anything after that was a bonus.

Tony: He was particularly good with strikers, probably because he'd been such a good one himself. Once I had this coach telling me to constantly find space, to always try and get free of the last defender, but I didn't like that. I told him that I liked having the defender right up against me. That way, I always knew where he was and when the ball came to me, I knew where to go to get away from him.

Clough came over and said, "Fantastic, young man. That's what I used to do. That's what all good centre-forwards should do." As a young player learning your trade, having a manager who understands your position so well was a huge boost.

Viv: He saw things in John Robertson that no one else did. In his autobiography he says that Robbo was fat, greasy and covered in chip fat when he first saw him and ... actually, he's still fat, greasy and covered in chip fat! He'll never change! But what a football brain he had. People ask if he could play today and I reckon he could.

Tony: He was a good player, Robbo. Everyone knew he was talented, arguably the most technically gifted midfielder at the club. His only problem was that he was a bit round and a bit slow. They'd try to play him inside before Clough arrived, but the first thing Brian did was whack him out wide. He was a revelation. If he'd have played for Barcelona or Manchester United, he'd be recognised as one of the finest wingers of all time. Clough never asked anyone to change, he just made it clear what was expected and gave praise where it was due. It gave Robbo the confidence to fulfil his potential.

Viv: He just made him believe in himself. If you want to define Brian Clough then that's where you go. He was the best at getting the most out of average players. If it wasn't for him instilling the belief in us, we'd never have made it. John Robertson would have drifted through his career as an "alright" footballer. Cloughie gave him the belief to win medals and represent his country.

Tony: Robbo's become a coach now. He always was a good judge of talent, Robbo, particularly when it was well-hidden. It's interesting that someone who needed an expert to spot the potential in him has now become that kind of expert for the next generation of players. He's certainly done very well working with Martin O'Neill.

Viv: He always was an intelligent lad though, underneath all of that. I'd never really describe him as a coach though. He's the buffer between the players and the manager. He's great at one-to-ones, telling people what he expects of them. I suppose he probably gets that from Clough as well, but I think we all have to a certain extent.

Tony: Clough was great for that. He'd sit down, talk to you, have some fun with you. Occasionally, he'd get some drinks in for everyone. Before the really big games, we'd always be together. We'd get a function room in the hotel.

Clough always said, "What the hell do you want to go to bed for? You'll never get any sleep, you've got a Cup Final tomorrow." Then he'd get the drinks in and him and his assistant Peter Taylor would start "The Clough & Taylor Show". They were hilarious. They'd just sit there telling stories and jokes, getting everyone involved in the banter. They were the ultimate after-dinner speakers. It put a smile on everyone's face and relaxed us. Then, usually at about midnight,

Clough would send us all to bed. "That's it, off you go," he'd say and we'd all troop off upstairs.

Viv: Taylor was vital. He would be your confidante; he'd look after you. Mind you, he'd also find out about you and find out what you liked. Then it would all end up going back to the boss!

Tony: Taylor had a gift. He could spot players and analyse them instantly. He looked at me and he said that I got kicked and pushed and elbowed but I always got up and he liked that. You know, it was the funny little things he'd see, the little mannerisms, the good things, rather than the bad things. You get so many scouts these days who say that their first job is to keep bad players away from the club. Taylor didn't care about that, he just wanted to bring good players in. I'm sure Kenny Burns won't mind me telling you what Taylor did to him before he signed. He had him followed! Kenny was a bit of a ruffian, apparently, so Taylor would get his flat cap on and go follow him around town to find out how rough he really was. He'd follow him to the pub, he'd follow him to the dog tracks, find out how much he was betting, how much he was losing. Can you imagine that happening now? Taylor was legendary for it. Him and Clough wanted all the information they could get before they signed some-one and they weren't afraid to go get it themselves. In all that time Kenny never knew he was being followed! It made us all wonder how much information they had on us.

Viv: It was a double act, Taylor and Clough, and you wouldn't see a better one anywhere in football.

Tony: They even rivalled Morecombe and Wise! When they weren't cracking jokes, they'd have a "Good Cop, Bad Cop" routine on the players. They used to constantly reverse the roles so you never knew what was going on. Martin O'Neill was a regular target because they knew that he'd get riled and try and defend himself. Peter would come in and shout, "Anyone could play right wing in this team, Martin, even the groundsman could do it!"

Martin would start arguing and then Cloughie would step in and say, "Come on, Pete. Martin does a lot of work round here, you know" and then Martin wouldn't know what to do. It had the rest of us in stitches. They'd prey on people's emotions and get them fired up, they were years ahead of their time in terms of simple man-management.

Viv: They were unique. In the aspect of the football side of it, the things they did were frightening, but it worked. Somehow it all came together.

Tony: People can say that Clough only succeeded when he had Taylor at his side, but I'm not sure that's the case. The driving force was always Brian Clough, there were probably influences other than Taylor's absence as to why things weren't going according to plan later on. Clough was the one who could be successful by himself and I'm not sure that Taylor could ever have matched him. They were a great partnership and Clough would be the first to say that. No one could spot a player like Taylor, but if you took them apart, as far as I'm concerned there was only one of them who was going to be a success and that would be Cloughie himself.

Viv: I think when Peter went out on his own, he struggled. I think they both needed one another. It was sad the way it finished. They had a row and stopped speaking and they didn't get a chance to make it up before Taylor died. I think Cloughie always regretted that. But when they were at their best, they were a force to be reckoned with. They improved us as players, so much so that we were able to play for our country.

Tony: When me and Viv got in the England squad the rest of the lads couldn't believe what we'd tell them about life at Forest.

Viv: The tradition was for the team to meet up in the White Hart pub in Cockfosters and we'd all have a couple of drinks and swap stories. It was tradition and it was like a club atmosphere. The Ipswich lads, the Liverpool lads and our lot, it was like home from home really. We'd start to talk about Clough and the things he'd done and they'd all be staring at us going, "Whaaaaat?"

Tony: They'd laugh, but there's an old video of Brian Clough in his early years and the things he was saying then, he was light years ahead of his time. He just kept it all simple for the players, took the pressure off and kept everyone in their place. He had control of everything from the goalkeeper to the tea lady.

Viv: He was ahead of his time in other ways as well. You see this 4–5–1 that everyone adopts to stop other teams outplaying them? Clough did that against Hamburg in the European Cup final. We had Gary Birtles up front, John Robertson wide left, Gary Mills wide right, packed the midfield, scored a goal on the counter attack and then just defended. He was far, far ahead of anyone else. You had respect for him. You'd run through a brick wall for him. It was the simplicity and it could still apply to today. Clough's ethos was right, he was spot on all the time. We were under instructions never to argue with referees and it was so clever. You're never going to make them change their minds so we must have ended up getting them on our side. Everyone in football knew that Cloughie's teams were respectful and they didn't moan and complain all the time. Over the course of time, that probably meant that we got decisions we wouldn't ordinarily get. Referees are only human, aren't they? In the whole scheme of things, he was very clever. People always want to talk about his drinking now though.

Tony: There wasn't any over the top drinking. Not when I was there.

Viv: In the later years, clearly there was. He was never drunk with us though. He used to say things, like the berating of people from the bench, where you would actually think of it as the ranting and raving of someone who's pissed. But then come half-time, he would be absolutely calm, absolutely straight. It wasn't drink. I think it was more the fact that he was always on that line in life that separates genius from ... I don't know ... whatever you want to call it!

Tony: But Cloughie was Cloughie. Friday before the game, we'd have a team meeting at lunch and we'd all have a drink. He'd get David Needham in front of the squad in the boardroom when he first signed him, Peter Shilton, likewise, when he first signed him and say to them "Right you. I've just paid a lot of money for you and these over here are some class players. Why don't you get us all a drink?" And off they'd go behind the bar and get the drinks in.

Viv: How can you argue with that?

Tony: I had a knock on my hotel door one Friday night and it was Kenny Burns.

"Tony," he says. "The boss wants to see us downstairs in the bar in five minutes."

I said, "It's Friday night! It's the night before the game!"

"Five minutes," he said.

Viv: I had the same thing!

Tony: So we get dressed and head down to the bar. Cloughie's there and he looks us up and down and says, "Right lads, what are we having?" We were playing West Brom in the Quarter-Finals of the Cup!

So anyway I said, "Alright, I'll have a beer."

Viv: We had to!

Tony: But John Robertson says, "I don't like beer."

Cloughie goes, "What do you like?"

"Dry martini and lemonade."

He says to the barman, "Get Mr Robertson a dry martini and lemonade," and he looks over at Archie Gemmill who's got a face like thunder. "What about you, Mr Gemmill?"

He says, "I only drink Dom Perignon."

So Clough turns to the barman and says, "Get a bottle of Dom Perignon for Mr Gemmill."

Viv: He wanted us all to tell a joke before the end of the night! It was gone midnight when we went to bed and we all woke up with headaches!

Tony: Expect the unexpected!

Viv: We played Celtic in the UEFA Cup, after Tony had left, and we drew in the first leg at the City Ground. All the Celtic fans were telling us that the game was up, they'd never lost a European tie at Parkhead. So the game was on the Wednesday and we all met at the airport on Monday morning. We fly to Glasgow and get on the coach, going through town. Suddenly the coach pulls up at this pub.

Cloughie says, "Right, everyone off, we're going for a drink."

So off we get and that afternoon we have four pints each! Two days before this vital second leg game. We all thought it was a bit strange but no one was arguing! As we filed out of the pub some time later, I was right behind Cloughie. I heard him turn to the barman and say, "Give that bill to your boss." And then he walked out. I thought that was strange. I mean there was about 20 of us all drinking four pints each, so it was quite a bit of money. It was only later that we found it was David Hay, the Celtic manager's pub. Cloughie's found out he's got a bar, done his research and then headed down to make his presence known! Anyway, we come down at 10am the next day for training, this is Tuesday remember, the day before the game, and we get on the coach. We end up driving for about ten minutes to this marina.

We're all like, "I can't see a fucking football pitch anywhere!" He takes us in there and there's this big bar, pool table, table tennis table all of that.

He says, "Pool table. Darts. Dominoes. Bar. We'll pick you up at 6pm." Then he walks out. You can imagine the state we were in at the end of that! He came and picked us up, we managed dinner in the hotel at night time and then we had to report for training on the morning of the game. Everyone comes down in their kit and he stands in front of us and says, "No training today."

Now, I'm one of the senior players by this point and I said, "Boss, we've done nothing since Saturday. We've been drinking for the last two days. We need to do some training."

He said, "Young man, you're right." Now we're staying at the hotel on Troon golf course. So he points to this bunker about 50 yards away. "You see that, gentlemen? I want you to run to it and run back again."

So everyone sprints over to the bunker and back, all desperate to run some of the shit off they've been drinking in the last couple of days, and we stand in front of him again.

"Right lads, now bed," he says.

We went to bed that afternoon and we beat them 2–1 later that night!

Tony: You can't imagine Arsene Wenger doing that, can you?

Viv: He had his way of doing things. Maybe it was a way of relaxing us, maybe he knew that we were young lads who had bags of stamina, I don't know. But it won us two European Cups.

Tony: I never saw Clough the worse for wear though. There's been a lot of stories about what happened afterwards, but I don't know anything about that. We got him when he was sharp as hell, when he was at his prime. No one thought it would become a problem. There were stories coming out that suggested that drinking was having an effect, but we never saw that.

Viv: There was also all the stuff about him running the football club by fear!

Tony: It wasn't like that at all. You cannot win things if the players are scared and they wouldn't accept it anyway. He put a little bit of fear in there, but not to the extent that people were terrified of him. If that was the case, you wouldn't have the characters that you have now. We used to go out occasionally and break our curfews just like any other team.

Viv: Initially, when we got involved with him, we were young and we didn't know what to do with it all. No one ever fully understood him, no one at all, not even John McGovern who worked with him for years, but the older we got the more we began to read the mannerisms.

Tony: There was one time, a European Cup game in Zurich and we'd won, but Clough said that he didn't want anyone to go out that night. He put a curfew down and insisted that we stayed at the hotel. Anyway, me and Viv, and Martin O'Neill, we all decided we were going to make a break for it anyway!

Viv: But John Robertson actually was too scared! He was there saying, "The manager will kill us!"

Tony: To be fair, he did want to come with us, but he got cold feet!

Viv: We were whispering at him, "You coward!"

Tony: I'll always remember sneaking out of that hotel in the dead of night, giggling away, walking down the path and then turning back to see this sad figure in the one lit window, looking down and waving at us. Poor Robbo! He really wanted to come, but he just got too scared! We raised a toast to him when we got to the bar!

Viv: We did one pre-season trip abroad where I got really lucky. We'd been out at lunch and I'd got absolutely lamped! I came back to the hotel and crashed out in bed, fast asleep. Cloughie had come in to see me about something and seen me snoring away. He didn't know I was pissed. Anyway, later that evening we're all at the team meeting and he points at me.

"You should all take the example of young Anderson there. He was in his bed this afternoon getting his rest for the next game, not like you lot out on the piss."

They slaughtered me for that!

Tony: And there's the one about the apprentices, remember?

Viv: Oh yes! These lads are in the dressing room cleaning boots and the phone goes. One of the youngsters picks it up and it's Cloughie.

"Four teas in my office, young man," he says.

"Piss off," says the apprentice.

"Do you know who this is?" asked Cloughie.

"Yeah," says the lad defiantly. "But do you know who this is?"

And there's a pause on the other end of the line because Cloughie hasn't got a clue.

"No?" says the boy. "Piss off then," and he puts the phone down! And he never got found out!

Tony: Mind you, there is another story though that might tell you a bit about him. I was getting married and the wedding was in the middle of the season. I plucked up the courage and went to see him.

"I'm getting married, boss. Is it possible to have the day off?"

Not only did he give me the day off but he gave me a few days off, booked the honeymoon in Jersey and paid for it himself.

He said, "No, you're not having a day off, you're having a few. You go away and enjoy yourself."

Paid for the whole thing.

Viv: He was a huge part of our lives. Prior to his arrival we were football nomads. He came in and gave us the belief, made us reach our potential. I think we all owe him a lot for that. I got a call from a journalist on the morning that he died. We weren't sure if it was true or not, but when it was finally confirmed I got on the phone and told the boys what had happened. It was a great shame, very sad.

Tony: Just before he died, there was this tribute evening for him in Nottingham. He got up to do a speech and he pointed at all of us on the same table as him.

"That lot over there," he said, "they used to do what I said. Now I class them as my friends and I'm proud to be associated with them."

That was the last time I saw him. The day he died, Viv called me to let me know. I was on a boat out to sea. It was a huge shock, it really was. You always thought he was going to go out on his toes. We saw him at this dinner and he looked fantastic, so it was a big shock.

Viv: I was supposed to go to that evening but I was away in Singapore. The last time I saw him was at a book signing in Middlesbrough and I had a chat with him there, but I'll always remember seeing him when I was at Sheffield Wednesday. By now I was getting to the age where I really had to do my warm-ups and, as captain, I was taking the boys out and organising it all. So I was out there for about ten minutes and then I walked off the pitch to the dressing room.

"Oi!" I heard from the side of the pitch. I looked over and

there he was, sat in the dugout on his own. So all the crowd are congregating around and pointing at him and he's going, "Come here, you."

"I'm just going in, Mr Clough," I said. "I've got to get ready for this game."

"Come here!" he said. "Give us a kiss."

Everybody's looking, so I can't do anything. He gets hold of me and gives me a big smacker in front of everyone! Ah, but it was always a great honour to see him.

Tony: What can you say about him? Me and Viv had him when we were very young and the thing you'll find with a lot of his former players is that they all say they were brought up on his values. The way you played football, the way you conducted yourself on and off the pitch, the way you lived your lives. All of the people from that era, all of the people that lived those values, you can trust them with anything.

Viv: You should have seen the array of players that turned out for his funeral. If those players came out on the transfer market now, there wouldn't be enough money to buy them. What a collection of talent he'd worked with.

Tony: It's always been said that Clough would have problems these days with the big name players and the money in the game, but I don't hold with that. Great players of yesteryear would be great now and I think it's the same with managers.

Viv: He wouldn't be able to do everything now the way he did then though. He'd be able to motivate the players, to build them into a team and to win things, but I think the rest of the game, the press, the agents, the stuff off the pitch, that would drive him crackers. He knows players and what they should or shouldn't do, but the press intrusion in his life would have been intolerable.

Tony: He'd have to adapt, certainly, but he would have been as successful today as he was back then. No one else could ever do what he did. Some of his former players have tried, but it will never work. There'll only ever be one Brian Clough.

Brian Clough died of stomach cancer in September 2004 at the age of 69. He had battled ill health for several years after retiring as Nottingham Forest manager at the end of the 1992/93 season.

Tony Woodcock left the City Ground for Cologne in 1979. He stayed until after the 1982 World Cup, when he returned to England and signed for Arsenal. He was the Gunners' top goal-scorer for four consecutive seasons before moving back to Germany.

Woodcock turned to coaching and later became Director of Football at Eintracht Frankfurt. He speaks fluent German and divides his time between there, England and Dubai. He has also worked for the FA as a consultant, notably on their preparations for the 2006 World Cup.

Viv Anderson was one of the final European Cup winners to leave Nottingham Forest, staying on until 1984 before teaming up with Woodcock again at Highbury. He was one of Alex Ferguson's first signings at Manchester United and enjoyed three years at Old Trafford before a move to Sheffield Wednesday and then Barnsley. He was briefly the manager at Oakwell before leaving to team up with Bryan Robson at Middlesbrough. He spent seven years at the Riverside Stadium as assistant manager, leaving with Robson in 2001.

Nottingham Forest were relegated in 1993. Despite bouncing straight back up with Clough's former player Frank Clark, they lasted just three years before crashing back down again. Another return to the big time followed, but this lasted just one season. The twice European Cup winners circled the drain until 2005 when they were relegated to the wastelands of the third flight.

After Clough's death, newspapers and internet message-boards were deluged with messages and tributes, but before he died Clough said that he didn't want anything of the sort.

"I want no epitaphs of profound history and all that type of thing," he said. "I contributed. I would hope they would say that, and I would hope somebody liked me."

Tony Woodcock and Viv Anderson run the sports consultancy firm, My Sports. You can find more information on them at www.mygroup direct.com.